PREFACE

1. Scope

This publication provides doctrine for joint electromagnetic spectrum management operations organization, planning, preparation, execution, and assessment in support of joint operations.

2. Purpose

This publication has been prepared under the direction of the Chairman of the Joint Chiefs of Staff. It sets forth joint doctrine to govern the activities and performance of the Armed Forces of the United States in joint operations and provides the doctrinal basis for interagency coordination and for US military involvement in multinational operations. It provides military guidance for the exercise of authority by combatant commanders and other joint force commanders (JFCs) and prescribes joint doctrine for operations and training. It provides military guidance for use by the Armed Forces in preparing their appropriate plans. It is not the intent of this publication to restrict the authority of the JFC from organizing the force and executing the mission in a manner the JFC deems most appropriate to ensure unity of effort in the accomplishment of the overall objective.

3. Application

a. Joint doctrine established in this publication applies to the joint staff, commanders of combatant commands, subunified commands, joint task forces, subordinate components of these commands, and the Services.

b. The guidance in this publication is authoritative; as such, this doctrine will be followed except when, in the judgment of the commander, exceptional circumstances dictate otherwise. If conflicts arise between the contents of this publication and the contents of Service publications, this publication will take precedence unless the Chairman of the Joint Chiefs of Staff, normally in coordination with the other members of the Joint Chiefs of Staff, has provided more current and specific guidance. Commanders of forces operating as part of a multinational (alliance or coalition) military command should follow multinational doctrine and procedures ratified by the United States. For doctrine and procedures not ratified by the United States, commanders should evaluate and follow the multinational command's doctrine and procedures, where applicable and consistent with US law, regulations, and doctrine.

For the Chairman of the Joint Chiefs of Staff:

WILLIAM E. GORTNEY
VADM, USN
Director, Joint Staff

TABLE OF CONTENTS

EXECUTIVE SUMMARY
COMMANDER'S OVERVIEW

- **Gives an Overview of Joint Electromagnetic Spectrum Management Operations**

- **Covers International Electromagnetic Spectrum Management**

- **Addresses National Defense Electromagnetic Spectrum Management**

- **Discusses Organizing for Joint Electromagnetic Spectrum Operations**

- **Explains Planning for Joint Electromagnetic Spectrum Operations**

- **Describes Conducting Joint Electromagnetic Spectrum Operations**

- **Provides Considerations for Multinational Operations**

Overview of Joint Electromagnetic Spectrum Management Operations

Joint electromagnetic spectrum management operations is a functional area ultimately responsible for coordinating electromagnetic spectrum access among multinational partners, throughout the operational environment.

Military operations are complicated by increasingly complex demands on the electromagnetic spectrum (EMS). All modern forces depend on the EMS. The EMS is a physical medium through which joint forces conduct operations. The importance of the EMS and its relationship to the operational capabilities is the key focus of joint electromagnetic spectrum management operations (JEMSMO).

The Electromagnetic Spectrum

The EMS is a highly regulated and saturated natural resource. The EMS includes the full range of all possible frequencies of electromagnetic radiation.

Joint Electromagnetic Spectrum Operations

Joint electromagnetic spectrum operations (JEMSO) include all activities in military operations to successfully plan and execute joint or multinational operations in order to control the electromagnetic operational environment (EMOE). JEMSO is comprised of electronic warfare (EW) and JEMSMO and aims to exploit, attack, protect, and manage resources within the EMOE and resolve electromagnetic interference (EMI) in order to achieve the commander's objectives.

Joint Electromagnetic Spectrum Management Operations	JEMSMO is planning, coordinating, and managing joint use of the EMS through operational, engineering, and administrative procedures. The primary goal of JEMSMO is to enable EMS-dependent capabilities and systems to perform their functions in the intended environment without causing or suffering unacceptable interference.

International Electromagnetic Spectrum Management

All nations share the electromagnetic spectrum and reserve their sovereign right to its unlimited use.	At the international and national levels, the primary concern for the use of the EMS is economic and not military. All nations have a sovereign right to allocate the EMS as needed to support their national interests, but the successful conduct of operations requires the joint force commander (JFC) to work with the nation at issue to balance these rights with the need to maintain security of US and multinational forces.
International Telecommunications Union	To promote international telecommunications cooperation to support trade, transportation, communications, and mutual protection against interference, most countries have agreed to generally follow International Telecommunications Union Allocations, Standards and Radio Regulations for spectrum use.
Allied Electromagnetic Spectrum Management Authorities	When joint operations are conducted by an Allied force, it is necessary to understand spectrum management (SM) roles, responsibilities, and processes within the alliance. The US is a member of two long-standing organizations: The North Atlantic Treaty Organization and the Combined Communications–Electronics Board.

National Defense Electromagnetic Spectrum Management

National Electromagnetic Spectrum Authorities— Strategic Planning and Management of the Electromagnetic Spectrum	The Communications Act of 1934, as amended, governs radio EMS use in the US and its territories. The act established duality in SM in the US between the President for federal government stations and the Federal Communications Commission (FCC). The FCC regulates the spectrum use of non-federal operated radio stations, common carriers, and private organizations or individuals. By Executive Order 12016 of 1978, the President delegated his functions under the act to a new organization created as the National Telecommunications and Information Administration (NTIA) and placed them under the Secretary of Commerce.

National Spectrum Supportability

Commanders must be aware of the policy and processes for national spectrum supportability. This is especially important because critical events occurring within the homeland, such as weapons of mass destruction events or natural disasters, require the coordination of civil and federal local, state, and national authorities whose equipment may operate, by law, in different frequency bands.

United States Military Communications– Electronics Board

The US Military Communications–Electronics Board (MCEB) is the principal Department of Defense (DOD) coordinating agency for SM. The MCEB functions under the policies and directives of the Secretary of Defense and the Joint Chiefs of Staff. The MCEB guides the DOD in preparing and coordinating technical directives and agreements and in allocating spectrum allotments from the NTIA. Its mission is three-fold: coordinate between DOD components, between DOD and other government departments and agencies, and between DOD and foreign nations.

Defense Spectrum Organization

Defense Spectrum Organization (DSO) supports a full range of initiatives and activities, ranging from long-term planning and development of advanced SM technologies to on-site problem solving for warfighters in the field. DSO's facilities and elements include the Joint Spectrum Center, the Strategic Planning Office, the Business Management Office, and the Program Management Office for the Global Electromagnetic Spectrum Information System.

Joint Frequency Management Office

Each supported geographic combatant commander (GCC) establishes a command policy on how the spectrum is used in his or her area of responsibility (AOR), obtains clearance (or approval) from host nations for use of the spectrum (through existing coordination procedures), and ensures that assigned military forces are authorized sufficient use of the spectrum to execute their designated missions. To accomplish these tasks, each supported GCC establishes a joint frequency management office (JFMO), typically under the cognizance of the communications system directorate of a joint staff (J-6), to support joint planning, coordination, and control of the spectrum for assigned forces.

Joint Spectrum Management Element	At the joint task force (JTF) level, a joint spectrum management element (JSME) may be established. The JSME within a JTF may be assigned from the J-6 staff, from a component's staff, or from an external command.
Service Spectrum Management Authorities	The **Air Force** Spectrum Management Office (AFSMO) mission is to plan, provide, and preserve access to the EMS for the Air Force and selected DOD activities. The **Army** Spectrum Management Office (ASMO) is the Army Service-level office for all spectrum-related matters. The **Navy and Marine** Corps Spectrum Center (NMSC) coordinates SM policy and guidance and represents the Navy, and when required, the Marine Corps, in spectrum negotiations with civil, military, and national regulatory organizations. The **United States Coast Guard (USCG)** Spectrum Management and Telecommunications Policy Division, COMMANDANT (CG-652) Office is the USCG Service-level office for all spectrum-related matters. The National Guard Bureau (NGB) J-6/C4 spectrum management branch is the designated office within NGB responsible for planning and executing SM for assigned forces and providing support to the National Guard (NG) joint force headquarters–state (JFHQ-State) in communications with United States Northern Command (USNORTHCOM).

Organizing for Joint Electromagnetic Spectrum Operations

How joint forces are organized to plan and execute joint electromagnetic spectrum management operations is a prerogative of the joint force commander.	It is the responsibility of the combatant commander to establish and promulgate command-specific policy and guidance for EMS use, the joint restricted frequency list (JRFL) process, the joint communications–electronics operating instructions, software defined radio waveform implementation and sharing, and other processes or directives that uniquely apply to the area (e.g., radar restrictions). A JFMO is a permanent organization within the combatant command (CCMD). Each GCC organizes the JFMO in accordance with geographic and functional requirements.
Air Force	At each echelon of US Air Force organization responsible for JEMSMO, the communications staff officer, in coordination with the intelligence staff officer and operations staff officer, is responsible for planning and coordinating JEMSMO.

Army	At each echelon of Army organization responsible for electromagnetic spectrum management operations, the assistant chief of staff (ACOS), signal staff officer, in coordination with the ACOS, intelligence staff officer, and ACOS, operations staff officer, is responsible for planning and coordinating EMS operations.
Marine Corps	The Commandant of the Marine Corps is responsible for spectrum supportability, including system/equipment spectrum certification and the allocation, assignment, and protection of all radio frequencies within the Marine Corps. Marine Corps force commanders provide operating forces and capabilities in support of the JFC. Marine Corps forces, installations, organizations, and activities coordinate SM support with the JFC via their respective Marine Corps Service component.
Navy	The NMSC provides the Chief of Naval Operations spectrum supportability, including system/equipment spectrum certification and the allocation, assignment, and protection of all radio frequency (RF) within the Navy. The Deputy Chief of Naval Operations for Information Dominance has delegated the responsibility for spectrum supportability and the management of the RF spectrum to Navy Cyber Forces (NAVCYBERFOR). NAVCYBERFOR has established the NMSC as the center of excellence for day-to-day spectrum certification and RF SM in support of all Navy and Marine Corps activities.
Coast Guard	The Spectrum Management Division supports JEMSMO by having trained personnel well-versed in joint operations.
National Guard Bureau	The 54 NG JFHQ-States and territories are supported with frequency assignments by the ASMO through Army Frequency Management Office–Continental United States. Frequency assignments for daily Air National Guard aircraft and air support operations are supported by the AFSMO.

Planning for Joint Electromagnetic Spectrum Operations

Spectrum management is a complex mission area within modern military and civil operations that must be fully integrated with other aspects of joint	Coordination of military EMS use is largely a matter of coordinating with other staff functions (primarily the intelligence directorate of a joint staff [J-2] and operations directorate of a joint staff [J-3]) and components (to include multinational partners) that rely on the EMS to accomplish their mission. Like other aspects of joint operations, joint

operations in order to achieve its full potential for contributing to an operation's objectives.

SM uses centralized planning and decentralized execution. Since the Services provide most of the assets available in joint operations, **Service component SM planners must be integrated into the joint planning process.**

Planning Considerations

To use the spectrum successfully, all users must work together by exchanging vital spectrum information from the beginning of the joint planning process through an approved DOD data exchange architecture. Primarily, personnel assigned to the J-2, J-3, and J-6 staff sections plan, coordinate, and control joint military use of the EMS.

Planning Process

The planning process for JEMSMO is conducted within the joint operation planning process and is designed to produce the products necessary for the commander to make timely decisions and aid in course of action development. **JEMSMO planning activities include define policy and guidance, gather spectrum requirements, develop the spectrum requirements summary, define the electromagnetic operational environment, obtain spectrum resources, and develop the spectrum management plan.**

Coordination with Network Operations, Electronic Warfare, and Intelligence

The portion of overlap between network operations (NETOPS) and JEMSMO is between the frequency management portion of JEMSMO and the NETOPS essential task, DOD information networks management. NETOPS tools used to assign frequencies for the network should also determine the spectrum requirement (frequencies) for the network and provide this information to the spectrum manager in the approved DOD format. At CCMDs and subordinate unified commands, coordination for EW will normally be handled through the JFC's EW staff or the joint electronic warfare cell (EWC). The EWC may be assigned to the J-3 and normally consists of members from the primary staff sections, a fires officer, and an electromagnetic spectrum manager. In many cases, the JSME does not have adequate visibility or knowledge of intelligence sensors, platforms, or systems in order to accomplish accurate deconfliction. Integrating intelligence staff and entities in all JEMSMO and JSME planning activities is crucial to effective operations preparation. The JRFL is the primary mechanism that enables coordination with intelligence.

Major Operations and Campaigns Planning	Due to the magnitude of major operations, the planning activities that will pose the biggest challenges are gathering requirements and defining the EMOE. Major operations require that the JSME have representation from each of the Services in order to fully develop the spectrum database.
Homeland Defense/Defense Support of Civil Authorities Planning	The defense support of civil authorities (DSCA)/homeland defense (HD) mission requires an unprecedented level of interoperability and cooperation between federal, state, and local governments; civilian first responders; and the public. JFMO NORTH is the designated office within the USNORTHCOM AOR responsible for planning and execution of SM for DSCA/HD assigned forces.

Conducting Joint Electromagnetic Spectrum Operations

Concept of Control	The supported JFC holds the authority for assigning frequencies to users, usually through the JFMO/JSME. The JFMO/JSME may on occasion delegate frequency assignment authority to subordinate commands. Authority to assign use of a specific spectrum resource (use of allotment plans developed by the JFMO/JSME) should be delegated to the lowest level of command possible, consistent with the principles of sound SM, spectrum-use considerations, concept of operations (CONOPS), and priority of mission functions detailed in the respective Service or joint publications.
Interference Resolution	To ensure critical frequencies and spectrum-dependent systems are protected from unintentional interference due to friendly operations, the JFMO/JSME will perform an interference analysis of all spectrum requests against existing frequency assignments to identify and deconflict potential interference before making a new assignment. The JSME is responsible for the analysis and attempts to resolve incidents of unacceptable EMI.
Service Perspectives	The unique functionality of each of the Services promotes a different perspective of how to conduct JEMSMO. While these unique perspectives influence and dictate how they train and organize, successful JEMSMO requires that the Services operate in unison following a common construct.

Multinational Operations

Multinational Operations	Normally, when a multinational force is formed, there will be no previously agreed upon spectrum operations

procedures. This creates difficulties and causes delays with the planning, coordination, management, and execution of spectrum operations. Spectrum operations procedures used within alliances should be agreed upon in the earliest stages of planning.

Considerations in Multinational Operations

Operation plans and communications support plans should address coordination among spectrum users to achieve effective exchange of information, elimination of duplication of effort, and mutual support. Activities that should be addressed within the CONOPS include the organizational structure and processes used in a multinational environment, security concerns, spectrum data exchange requirements, and spectrum tools. For JEMSMO to be executed properly, spectrum operators must have a complete picture of their EMOE to populate spectrum databases and management tools. Due to security considerations related to the use or employment of some equipment that nations employ for military intelligence or other sensitive functions, some equipment information may not be releasable to all countries involved in an operation.

Considerations for Foreign Humanitarian Assistance/Disaster Relief

Military forces may be deployed to provide aid to the civil administration in a mix of civil and military humanitarian relief agencies. The civil administration (if one exists) should provide an SM framework for the deployed military force. Much of the JEMSMO would focus on host nation coordination and ensuring that disruption to civil systems would be minimized through coordination.

CONCLUSION

This publication provides doctrine for joint electromagnetic spectrum management operations organization, planning, preparation, execution, and assessment in support of joint operations.

CHAPTER I
OVERVIEW OF JOINT ELECTROMAGNETIC SPECTRUM MANAGEMENT OPERATIONS

1. Introduction

Military operations are complicated by increasingly complex demands on the electromagnetic spectrum (EMS). All modern forces depend on the EMS. The EMS is a physical medium through which joint forces conduct operations. EMS-dependent devices are used by both civilian and military organizations and individuals for intelligence; communications; position, navigation, and timing; sensing; command and control (C2); attack; ranging; chemical, biological, radiological, and nuclear (CBRN) sensor data collection/transmission; unmanned aircraft systems (UASs); civil infrastructure; data transmission and information storage and processing. The importance of the EMS and its relationship to the operational capabilities is the key focus of joint electromagnetic spectrum management operations (JEMSMO). JEMSMO is a functional area ultimately responsible for coordinating EMS access among multinational partners, throughout the operational environment.

a. The Electromagnetic Spectrum

(1) The EMS is a physics-based maneuver space essential to control the operational environment during all military operations. Information and data exchange between platforms and capabilities will at some point rely on the EMS for transport. This maneuver space is constrained by both military and civil uses as well as adversary attempts to deny the use of the EMS, creating a congested and contested environment. This constrains freedom of maneuver to use all capabilities of friendly forces throughout the operational environment (see Figure I-1).

(2) The EMS is a highly regulated and saturated natural resource. The EMS (Figure I-2) includes the full range of all possible frequencies of electromagnetic (EM) radiation. Frequency refers to the number of occurrences of a periodic event over time. For radio frequencies (RFs), this is expressed in cycles per second or hertz (Hz). Generally, the frequencies between 30 Hz and 300 gigahertz are referred to as the RF spectrum.

(3) While this publication focuses primarily on the RF portion of the EMS, it should be noted that emergent technologies, capabilities, and systems (e.g., free space optics, infrared and laser technologies, and electronic warfare [EW] devices) are under development and being fielded that operate across the RF and non-RF portions of the EMS and must be considered. As the RF portion of the spectrum becomes more saturated, it can be expected that the use of higher frequencies will be developed to support communications, intelligence, and weapons systems and capabilities, and require planning and management.

b. Electromagnetic Operational Environment

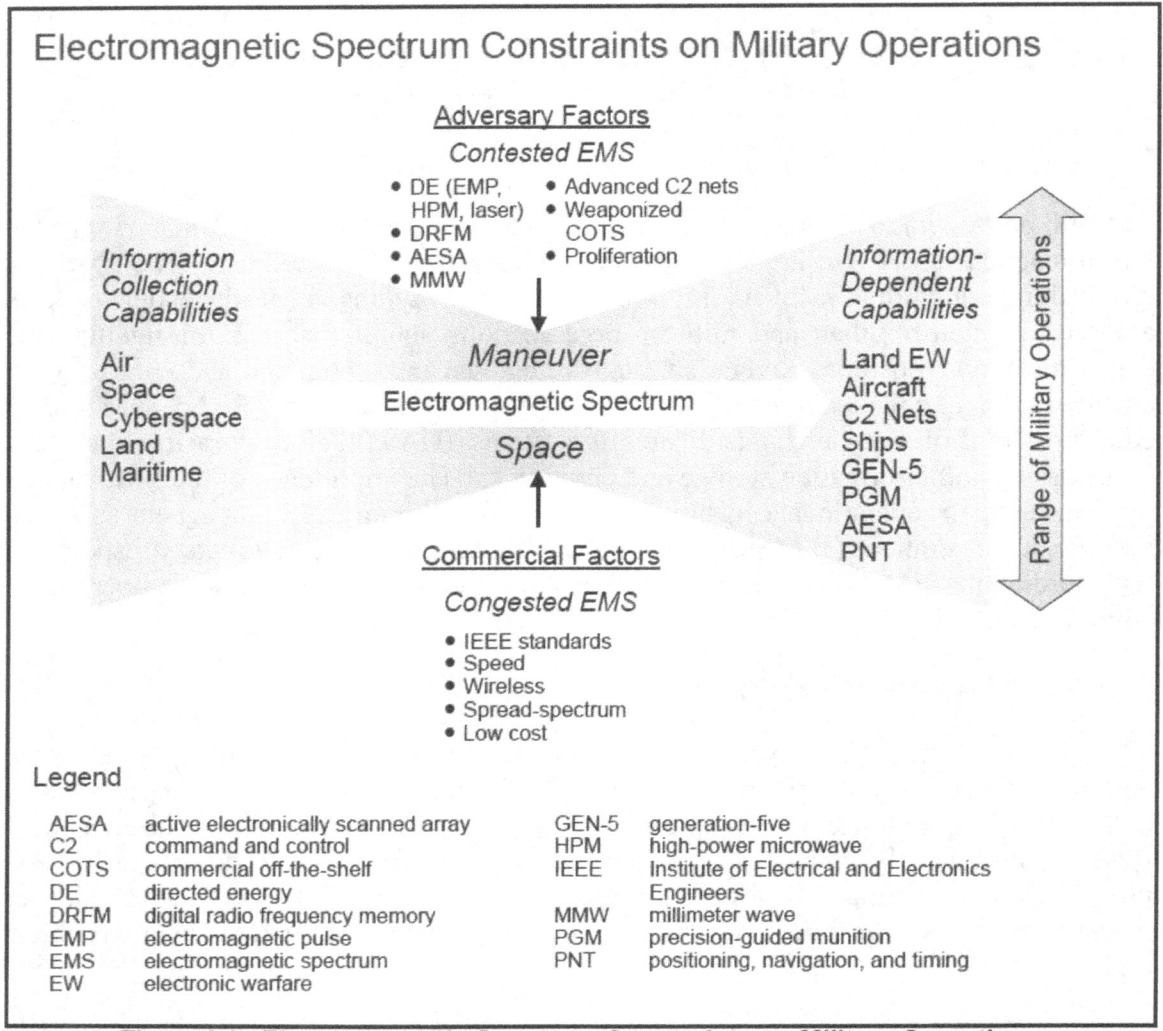

Figure I-1. Electromagnetic Spectrum Constraints on Military Operations

(1) Joint Publication (JP) 3-0, *Joint Operations*, states the operational environment is the composite of the conditions, circumstances, and influences that affect employment of capabilities and bear on the decisions of the commander. It encompasses physical areas and factors (of the air, land, maritime, and space domains) and the information environment (which includes cyberspace). The joint force commander (JFC) defines these areas with geographical boundaries in order to facilitate coordination, integration, and deconfliction of joint operations among joint force components and supporting commands. One goal of the JFC is to shape and control the electromagnetic operational environment (EMOE) within the EMS. However, the EMS transcends all physical domains and the information environment and extends beyond defined borders or boundaries, thus complicating the joint electromagnetic spectrum operations (JEMSO). A variety of factors, including the types of equipment employed, users of the equipment (e.g., air, naval, and land forces), adversary capabilities, geography, and weather also significantly influence the conduct of JEMSMO (see Figure I-3).

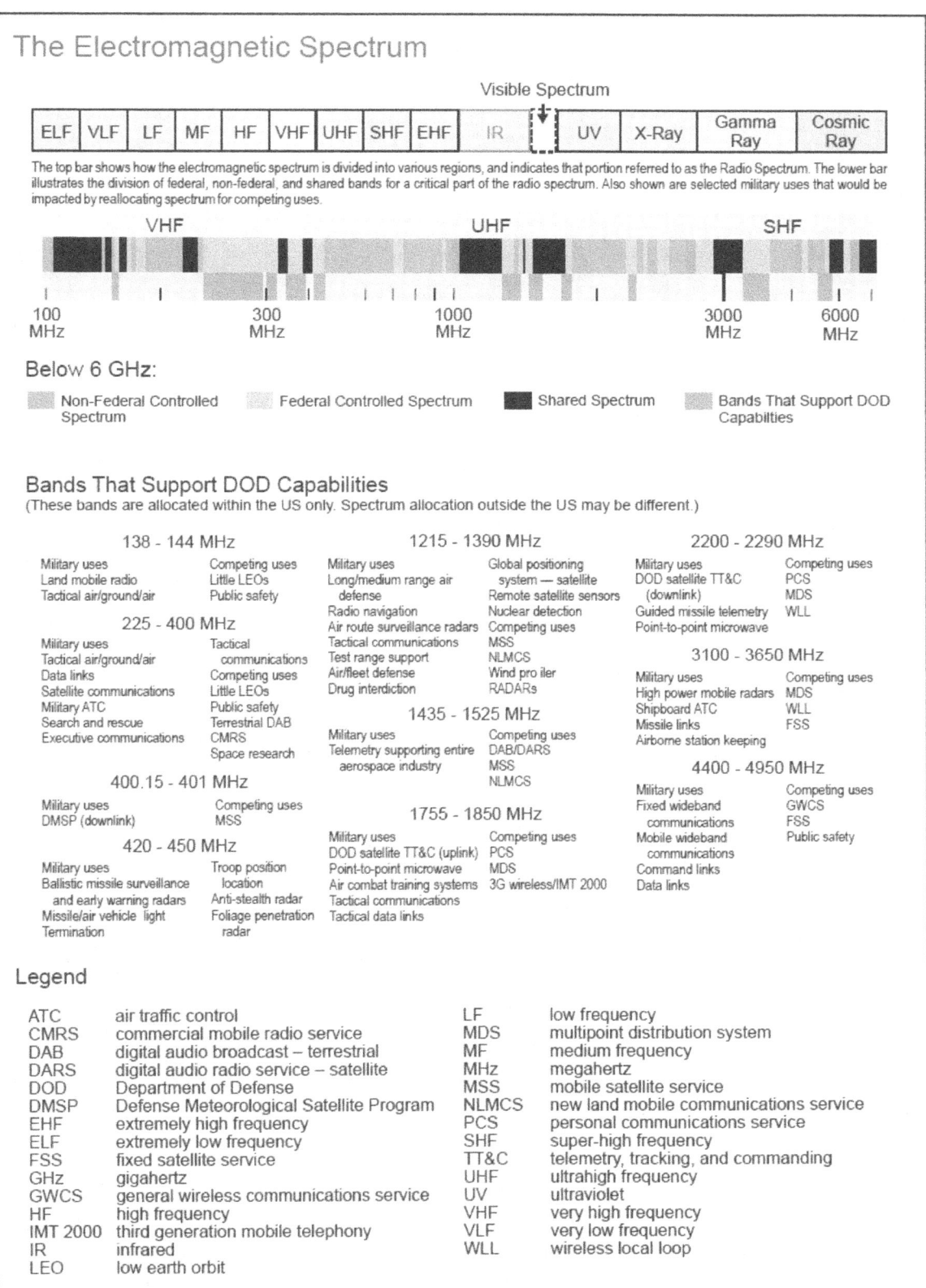

The Electromagnetic Spectrum

Visible Spectrum

| ELF | VLF | LF | MF | HF | VHF | UHF | SHF | EHF | IR | | UV | X-Ray | Gamma Ray | Cosmic Ray |

The top bar shows how the electromagnetic spectrum is divided into various regions, and indicates that portion referred to as the Radio Spectrum. The lower bar illustrates the division of federal, non-federal, and shared bands for a critical part of the radio spectrum. Also shown are selected military uses that would be impacted by reallocating spectrum for competing uses.

VHF   UHF   SHF

100 MHz   300 MHz   1000 MHz   3000 MHz   6000 MHz

Below 6 GHz:

Non-Federal Controlled Spectrum   Federal Controlled Spectrum   Shared Spectrum   Bands That Support DOD Capabilties

Bands That Support DOD Capabilities
(These bands are allocated within the US only. Spectrum allocation outside the US may be different.)

138 - 144 MHz

Military uses	Competing uses
Land mobile radio	Little LEOs
Tactical air/ground/air	Public safety

225 - 400 MHz

Military uses	Tactical
Tactical air/ground/air	communications
Data links	Competing uses
Satellite communications	Little LEOs
Military ATC	Public safety
Search and rescue	Terrestrial DAB
Executive communications	CMRS
	Space research

400.15 - 401 MHz

| Military uses | Competing uses |
| DMSP (downlink) | MSS |

420 - 450 MHz

Military uses	Troop position
Ballistic missile surveillance	location
and early warning radars	Anti-stealth radar
Missile/air vehicle light	Foliage penetration
Termination	radar

1215 - 1390 MHz

Military uses	Global positioning
Long/medium range air	system — satellite
defense	Remote satellite sensors
Radio navigation	Nuclear detection
Air route surveillance radars	Competing uses
Tactical communications	MSS
Test range support	NLMCS
Air/fleet defense	Wind pro iler
Drug interdiction	RADARs

1435 - 1525 MHz

Military uses	Competing uses
Telemetry supporting entire	DAB/DARS
aerospace industry	MSS
	NLMCS

1755 - 1850 MHz

Military uses	Competing uses
DOD satellite TT&C (uplink)	PCS
Point-to-point microwave	MDS
Air combat training systems	3G wireless/IMT 2000
Tactical communications	
Tactical data links	

2200 - 2290 MHz

Military uses	Competing uses
DOD satellite TT&C	PCS
(downlink)	MDS
Guided missile telemetry	WLL
Point-to-point microwave	

3100 - 3650 MHz

Military uses	Competing uses
High power mobile radars	MDS
Shipboard ATC	WLL
Missile links	FSS
Airborne station keeping	

4400 - 4950 MHz

Military uses	Competing uses
Fixed wideband	GWCS
communications	FSS
Mobile wideband	Public safety
communications	
Command links	
Data links	

Legend

ATC	air traffic control	LF	low frequency
CMRS	commercial mobile radio service	MDS	multipoint distribution system
DAB	digital audio broadcast – terrestrial	MF	medium frequency
DARS	digital audio radio service – satellite	MHz	megahertz
DOD	Department of Defense	MSS	mobile satellite service
DMSP	Defense Meteorological Satellite Program	NLMCS	new land mobile communications service
EHF	extremely high frequency	PCS	personal communications service
ELF	extremely low frequency	SHF	super-high frequency
FSS	fixed satellite service	TT&C	telemetry, tracking, and commanding
GHz	gigahertz	UHF	ultrahigh frequency
GWCS	general wireless communications service	UV	ultraviolet
HF	high frequency	VHF	very high frequency
IMT 2000	third generation mobile telephony	VLF	very low frequency
IR	infrared	WLL	wireless local loop
LEO	low earth orbit		

Figure I-2. The Electromagnetic Spectrum

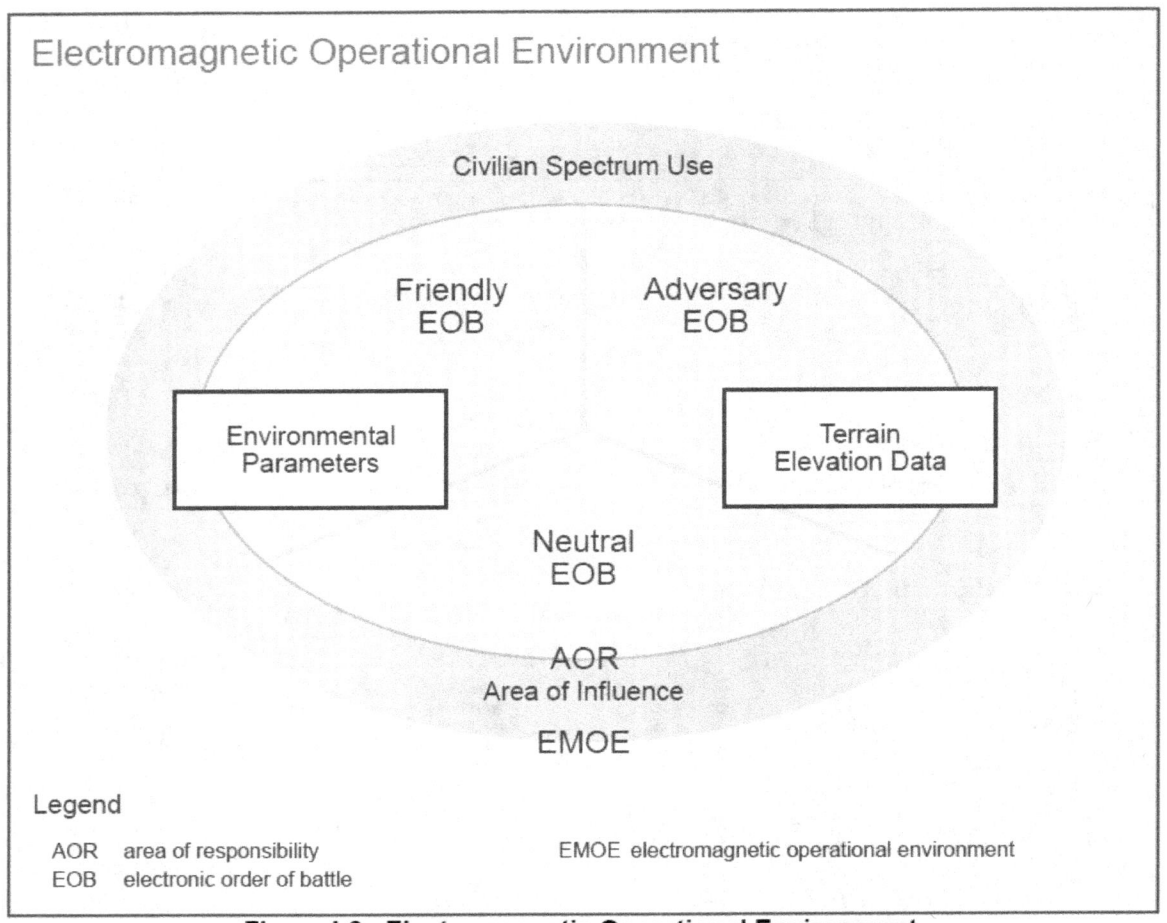

Figure I-3. Electromagnetic Operational Environment

(2) The electromagnetic environment (EME) is described as the resulting product of the power and time distribution, in various frequency ranges, of the radiated or conducted EM emission levels encountered by a military force, system, or platform when performing its assigned mission in its intended operational environment. It is the sum of electromagnetic interference (EMI); electromagnetic pulse (EMP); hazards of EM radiation to personnel, ordnance, and volatile materials; and natural phenomena effects of lightning and precipitation static. Essentially, the EME is the global EM background.

(3) EMOE is composed of the background EME and the friendly, neutral, and adversarial electronic order of battle (EOB) within the EM area of influence associated with a given operational area. This is the portion of the EME where JEMSMO is conducted at a given time.

(4) Different systems require different frequencies to operate effectively. Jungle, urban, or harsh climatic environments can all have adverse effects on spectrum-dependent systems. Additionally, some frequencies, such as super-high frequencies used for satellite communications, are adversely affected by fog, rain, or snow. Systems that use high frequency (HF) for propagation are affected by solar activities, such as sunspots and solar

flares, in addition to atmospheric fluctuations. Lastly, all systems are subject to man-made interference from other transmitters, power lines, or static electricity.

c. **Joint Electromagnetic Spectrum Operations**

(1) JEMSO include all activities in military operations to successfully plan and execute joint or multinational operations in order to control the EMOE.

(2) JEMSO is comprised of EW and JEMSMO and aims to exploit, attack, protect, and manage resources within the EMOE and resolve EMI in order to achieve the commander's objectives. It enables EMS-dependent systems to perform their functions in the intended operational environment. JEMSO enables and supports the six joint functions of C2, intelligence, fires, movement and maneuver, protection, and sustainment. See Figure I-4).

d. **Joint Electromagnetic Spectrum Management Operations**

(1) JEMSMO is planning, coordinating, and managing joint use of the EMS through operational, engineering, and administrative procedures. The primary goal of JEMSMO is to enable EMS-dependent capabilities and systems to perform their functions in

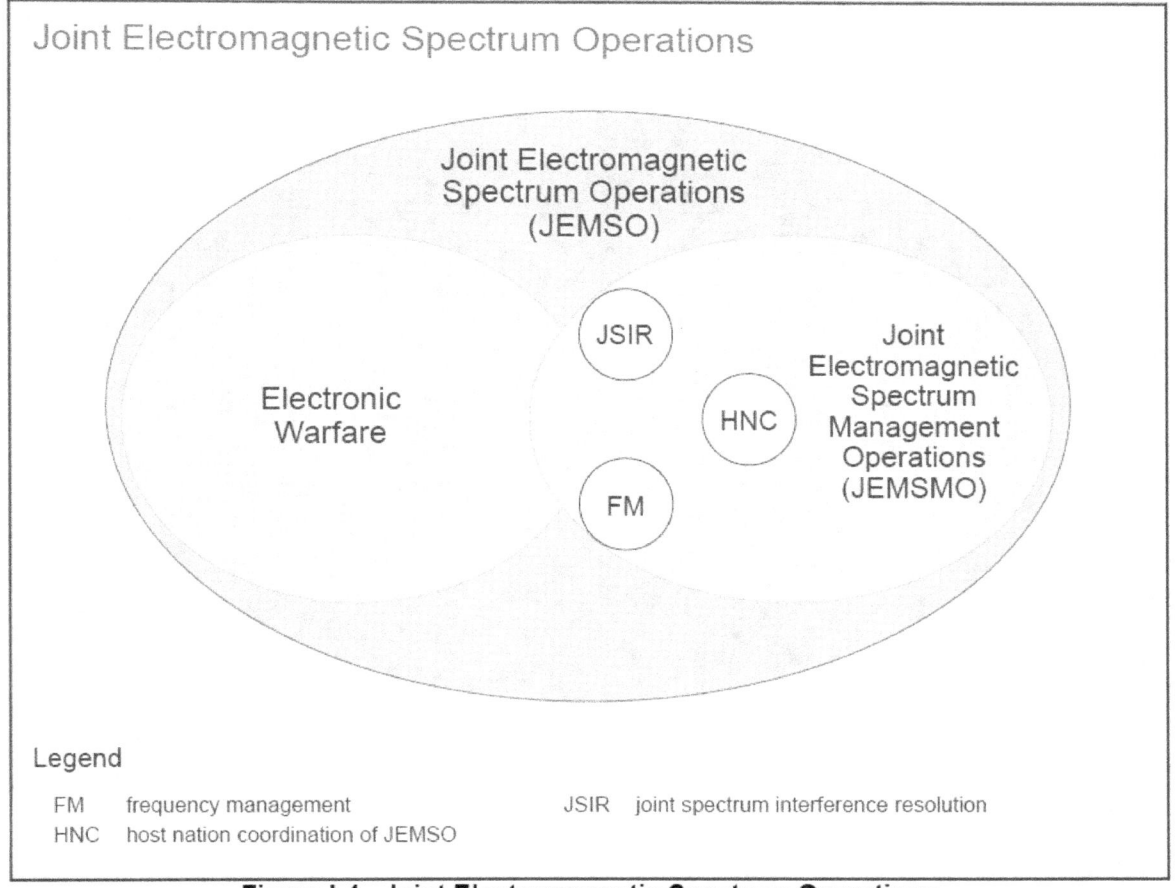

Figure I-4. Joint Electromagnetic Spectrum Operations

the intended environment without causing or suffering unacceptable interference. The secondary goal is to utilize the available EMS in the most efficient and effective manner while accomplishing the mission by using technical policy and techniques available to the electromagnetic spectrum manager (EMSM).

(2) JEMSMO is composed of three interrelated functions: frequency management (FM), host nation coordination (HNC), and joint spectrum interference resolution (JSIR). Together, these functions enable the planning, management, and execution of JEMSMO. Figure I-5 depicts the JEMSMO construct.

(3) By maintaining situational awareness of the EMOE, the commander is able to shape the environment by protecting, exploiting, attacking, sensing, and communicating through the EMS.

e. **Spectrum Management**

(1) Inherent within JEMSMO is spectrum management (SM). SM is the planning, coordinating, and managing joint use of the EMS through operational, engineering, and administrative procedures. The objective of SM is coordinated, prioritized, and deconflicted

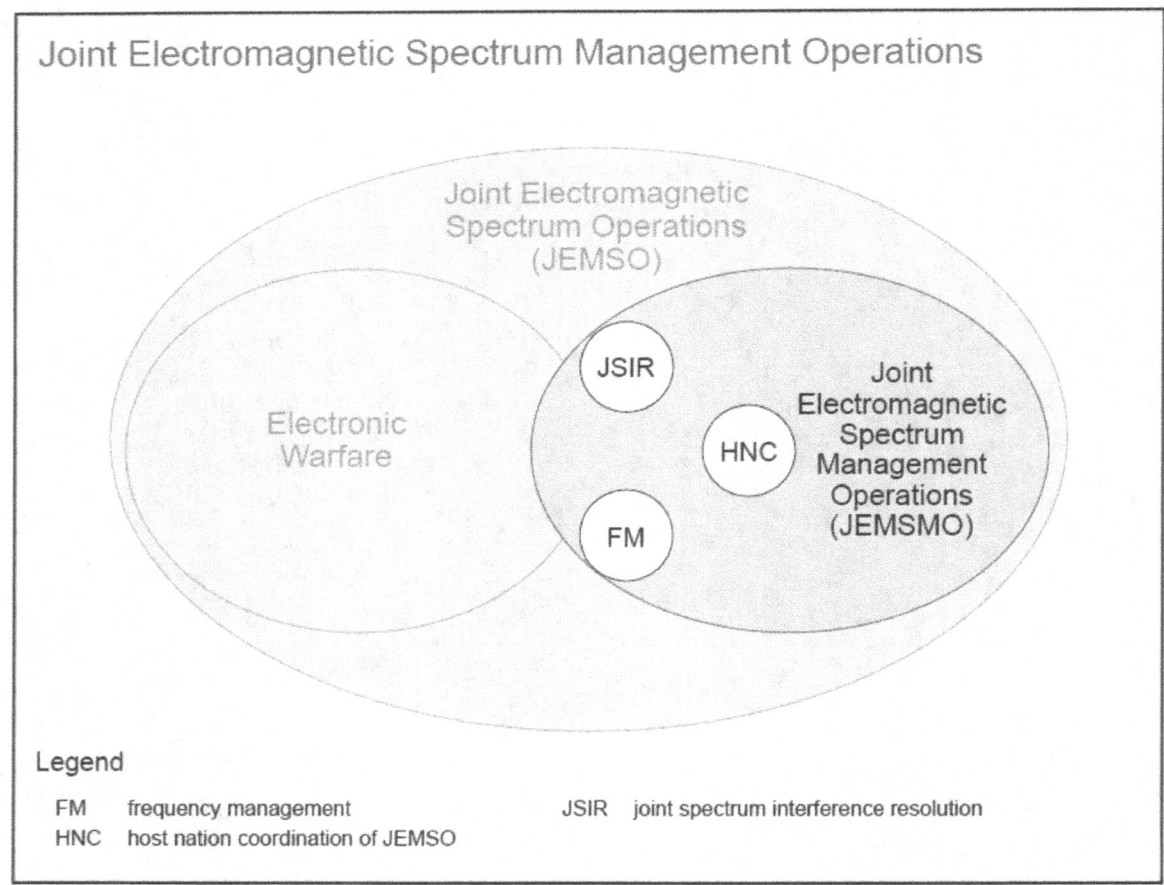

Figure I-5. Joint Electromagnetic Spectrum Management Operations

operations for EMS-dependent systems without causing or suffering unacceptable interference.

(2) EMS-dependent capabilities and systems throughout the strategic, operational, and tactical levels compete for the limited resources of EMS. SM provides the planning framework for the use of the EMS. This is a continuous process accomplished by:

(a) Defining the policy and guidance necessary to plan, manage, and execute JEMSMO.

(b) Gathering requirements for EMS-dependent capabilities and systems.

(c) Developing the EMS requirements summary used to quantify the frequencies and bandwidths necessary to support the operation or mission.

(d) Defining and characterizing the EMOE, thus establishing the common source of EMS management information.

(e) Developing the SM plan to establish specific guidance and procedures for managing, requesting, coordinating, and assigning EMS use.

(f) Integrating EW EMS requirements with friendly EMS-dependent systems and capabilities to ensure that systems can operate within their intended environment.

f. **Frequency Management.** FM encompasses requesting, nominating, conducting interference analysis, coordinating, assigning, and promulgating frequencies for EMS-dependent capabilities and systems. It allows for access to the EMS and protection of capabilities from harmful interference. FM also provides the frequency assignments to support development of the joint communications–electronics operating instructions (JCEOI) and joint restricted frequency list (JRFL). Examples of FM include providing the frequencies for assignment to radios on specific platforms, providing frequencies for UASs, and providing the frequencies for communications networks.

g. **Host Nation Coordination**

(1) HNC is the activity to obtain authorization to operate EMS-dependent systems within a sovereign nation. HNC pertains to foreign nations as well as the US and its territories. Granting approval to operate within a country is a sovereign right held by that country.

(2) HNC is normally accomplished through procedures established by geographic combatant commander (GCC) agreements with host nations (HNs). HNC should be conducted, when appropriate, with all countries in the area of interest (AOI). The unauthorized use of the EMS in HNs may be considered a violation of international treaty or law or local laws and regulations, and the JFC, subordinate commanders, or operators may be held criminally or financially liable for violations and may have equipment confiscated.

h. **Interference Resolution.** JSIR is the activity to identify, report, analyze, and mitigate or resolve incidents of EMI. JSIR is a continuous activity once forces have deployed and is not part of the planning process. JSIR is required to allow for protection of friendly EMS-dependent systems. Incidents of EMI will be resolved or mitigated at the lowest possible level within the command structure. EMI can be induced intentionally, as in some forms of EW, or unintentionally, as a result of spurious emissions and responses, and intermodulation products.

2. Electromagnetic Environmental Effects

a. Electromagnetic environmental effects (E3) impact the operational capability of military forces, equipment, systems, and platforms. They encompass all EM disciplines, including EM compatibility and EMI, EM vulnerability, EMP, electronic protection (EP), hazards of electromagnetic radiation to personnel (HERP), hazards of electromagnetic radiation to ordnance (HERO), hazards of electromagnetic radiation to fuels (HERF), and natural phenomena effects of lightning and precipitation static.

(1) The EME experienced by the joint force is continuously changing as existing systems are modified, new systems are installed, units move in closer proximity to each other, or natural phenomenon change. When platforms and associated systems and equipment (avionics, ordnance, fuel, etc.) are exposed to an operational EME different from those for which they were designed and tested, the potential for safety, interoperability, and reliability problems increases.

(2) JEMSMO requires a thorough regard for E3 through mitigation of interference and ensuring systems are electromagnetically compatible. Most system degradation encountered can be attributed to EMI. A substantial amount of planning and coordination is required to reduce the chances of EMI occurrences. This is particularly evident in joint operations where equipment, platforms, and personnel are continually moving and changing as operations evolve. Equipment designed for a specific environment or purpose but employed in a nontraditional role may present a particularly challenging situation. An example would be an Army helicopter landing on a Navy ship. This example presents a number of considerations. Among these considerations are whether the helicopter can communicate with the ship, will ship systems such as radars cause harmful effects to the avionics systems of the aircraft, or will the transmitters on the aircraft present a hazard to ordnance on the ship? This example highlights some specific examples of hazards that are addressed in the following paragraphs.

b. HERP is the potential hazard that exists when personnel are exposed to an EM field of sufficient intensity to heat the human body. Radar, communication systems, and EW systems which use high-power RF transmitters and high-gain antennas represent a biological hazard to personnel working on, or in the vicinity of, these systems. Therefore, stand-off areas around high-powered RF antennas should be clearly marked. Since it is not possible to visibly determine if an antenna is transmitting, personnel should avoid entering these stand-off areas at all times.

c. HERO is the danger of accidental actuation of electro-explosive devices or otherwise electrically activating ordnance because of RF EM fields. This unintended actuation could have safety (premature firing) or reliability (dudding) consequences. HERO may be induced through holes or cracks in the casing, wires, or fuses and is most susceptible during assembly, disassembly, loading, or unloading.

d. HERF is the potential hazard that is created when volatile combustibles, such as fuel, are exposed to EM fields of sufficient energy to cause ignition. HERF is most likely to occur when refueling operations are taking place. Care should be taken to separate fueling points and high-powered radar, radio, directed energy weapons, or jammers to reduce the possibility of RF induced arcs that could ignite fuel. Personnel must ensure proper grounding and static discharge procedures are adhered to and that RF transmissions be minimized or ceased during refueling operations.

e. **Electromagnetic Pulse.** The interaction of gamma radiation with the atmosphere can cause a short pulse of electric and magnetic fields that may damage and interfere with the operation of electrical and electronic equipment and can cause widespread disruption. EMP is one of the primary ways that a nuclear detonation produces its damaging effects. The effects of EMP can extend to hundreds of kilometers depending on the height and yield of a nuclear burst. A high-altitude electromagnetic pulse (HEMP) can generate significant disruptive field strengths over a continental-size area. The portion of the EMS most affected by EMP and HEMP is the radio spectrum. Planning for communication system protection is key when the potential for EMP is likely.

See Field Manual 3-11.4/Marine Corps Warfighting Publication (MCWP) 3-37.2/Navy Tactics, Techniques, and Procedures (NTTP) 3-11.27/Air Force Tactics, Techniques, and Procedures Instruction (AFTTP[I]) 3-2.46, Multi-Service Tactics, Techniques, and Procedures for Nuclear, Biological, and Chemical (NBC) Protection; *JP 3-11,* Operations in Chemical, Biological, Radiological, and Nuclear (CBRN) Environments; *and JP 3-41,* Chemical, Biological, Radiological, and Nuclear Consequence Management, *for detailed discussions of EMP considerations during military operations.*

f. E3 presents many unique challenges to JEMSMO, although most can be mitigated through proper planning and coordination. JEMSMO develops the mitigation strategies, such as special instructions, the JRFL, JCEOI, and spectrum plan, to minimize the impact of EME on operations in the operational area. Other mitigation strategies include using protected waveforms, which provide low probability of detection, reducing the potential for electronic attack (EA). Lastly, safety must always be considered when operating in the vicinity of high-powered RF emitters to avoid loss of life or equipment.

For more discussion on JRFL, see JP 3-13.1, Electronic Warfare.

3. Role of Electromagnetic Spectrum Management Operations in Joint and Multinational Operations

a. Military operations today are nearly always joint, and in many cases, involve multinational forces. The proper execution of JEMSMO enables the commander to not only command and control but also to gather intelligence, execute both lethal and nonlethal fires missions, move and maneuver forces, and protect and sustain the force. All of these functions are accomplished in a dynamic environment and require continual planning, coordination, and management of the EMS to ensure that the full complement of capabilities is at the commanders' disposal.

b. The EM portion of the network is a key enabler of the network-enabled force; commanders should understand that the EMS is not a replaceable resource like fuel or ammunition. Once the allotted EMS has been allocated to support specific capabilities or systems in a specific geographical area, it is no longer available for use. The commander may need to operationally assess the impact of sacrificing other potentially critical capabilities in order to use another (i.e., the use of C2 or counter radio-controlled improvised explosive device EW, the use of C2 or intelligence, surveillance, and reconnaissance). EMS can, however, be reallocated or reused, depending on distance and power between emitters.

4. Relationship to Other Mission Areas

a. **Information Operations (IO).** IO is the integrated employment, during military operations, of information-related capabilities in concert with other lines of operation to influence, disrupt, corrupt, or usurp the decision making of adversaries and potential adversaries while protecting our own. JEMSMO enables IO, primarily by ensuring that IO can be conducted with minimal EMI caused by friendly forces (frequency fratricide) and without negative E3. Lack of concise, preplanned frequency coordination may have an adverse effect on friendly users in the form of interference. JEMSMO supports and enables the coordination, integration, and synchronization of information-related capabilities through both the EM portion of the C2 channels and the various operational EMS requirements of these capabilities.

b. **Relationship to Military Information Support Operations (MISO).** JEMSMO supports and enables the joint MISO communications plan by ensuring that spectrum is available for both radio and broadcast services when these are controlled by the combatant commander (CCDR), such as in offensive operations. An example would be the employment of the Special Operations Media System-Broadcast that has a capability to provide local radio and television (TV) support. JEMSMO can also leverage MISO data repositories to validate EMS data. Of particular interest is the radio/TV collection. This collection has statistics on radio and TV facilities in various countries. It includes such information as location, equipment range, and frequencies, and users can search the collection based on facility characteristics.

For more discussion on MISO, see JP 3-13.2, Military Information Support Operations.

c. **Relationship to Military Deception (MILDEC) and Operations Security (OPSEC).** MILDEC and OPSEC are complementary activities. MILDEC is actions executed to deliberately mislead adversary military, paramilitary, or violent extremist organization decision makers, thereby causing the adversary to take specific actions (or inactions) that will contribute to the accomplishment of the friendly mission. OPSEC is a process that identifies critical information to determine if friendly actions can be observed by adversary intelligence systems, determines if information obtained by adversaries could be interpreted to be useful to them, and then executes selected measures that eliminate or reduce adversary exploitation of friendly critical information. JEMSMO support to MILDEC is concerned with ensuring that any plan that requires additional EMS support can be met, while OPSEC requirements are that sensitive information such as frequency plans, operational ranges of classified systems, and the JRFL information are safeguarded.

For more discussion on MILDEC and OPSEC, see JP 3-13.4, Military Deception, *and JP 3-13.3,* Operations Security.

d. **Relationship to Computer Network Operations (CNO).** CNO is used to attack, deceive, degrade, disrupt, deny, exploit, and defend electronic information and infrastructure. Like EW, CNO is highly sensitive, and EMS operators may not always have accurate situational awareness of planned or ongoing operations. CNO differs from EW in that EW concerns the use of radiated energy, whereas CNO is concerned with the information (data) on the network or the computers and networks themselves. CNO that require EMS support or protection must be coordinated and integrated in much the same way as EW missions. In order for JEMSMO to enable and support CNO, staffs must collaborate, plan, and share information to facilitate mission success.

e. **Relationship to Electronic Warfare**

(1) EW refers to any military action involving the use of EM or directed energy to control the EMS or to attack the enemy. EW includes three major subdivisions: EA, EP, and EW support. JEMSMO supports and enables the execution of EW through planning and coordinating use of the EMS in order to conduct JEMSMO and EW concurrently. As friendly EMS access is not assured, EW supports JEMSMO by denying adversary access and mitigating the effects of adversary EMS activity on friendly systems.

(2) SM must be an integral part of EW planning to ensure that the EM scheme of maneuver reduces, mitigates, or eliminates the effects of EW systems on the other elements of JEMSO. The proliferation of EA systems in the operational environment has made participation in EW planning critical for the EMSM. In addition to both airborne and terrestrial EA systems, other weapons that use EM radiation such as directed energy weapons must be taken into account.

(3) Coordination for EW will normally take place in the electronic warfare cell (EWC). The EWC is under the cognizance of the operations directorate of a joint staff (J-3) and normally consists of members from the primary staff sections, a fires officer, and an EMSM and is headed by the senior electronic warfare officer (EWO). The EMSM participates and represents JEMSMO issues. This includes providing an EW integration plan.

(4) The EWO uses the EOB to determine EA priorities and provides this to the EMSM for further analysis on the potential impact to other EMS users. This process requires information from the EA request, JRFL, JCEOI, and FM database. The analysis will determine what impact the EW mission will have on EMS activities, such as

communication nets, military systems, and adversary communications nets being exploited. The end product will be a JRFL that contains frequencies that can be protected during the execution of EA activities and publication of other EA guidance. This product is produced on an as-needed basis.

See Chapter V, "Planning Joint Electromagnetic Spectrum Operations," and Chapter VI, "Conducting Joint Electromagnetic Spectrum Operations," for more information on how the JRFL is developed and utilized. For additional discussion on the JRFL, see JP 3-13.1, Electronic Warfare.

(5) The EMS-use analysis forms the basis of an integrated EMS-use and maneuver plan. In some cases, EMS conflict identified during this analysis will be irresolvable, requiring the JFC to weigh the impact of EA employment on friendly force and civilian EMS use. As the EMOE is by definition a dynamic environment, EW and JEMSMO personnel work constantly to provide the JFC with the best employment of EMS-dependent systems while denying the adversary the same in order to accomplish the JFC's objectives.

f. **Relationship to Intelligence**

(1) JEMSMO is integral to the gathering, processing, and dissemination of intelligence. The EA request process is one mechanism used to coordinate and integrate EMS use between the commander's operational frequencies and those being exploited or protected so that the full spectrum of intelligence operations can be conducted.

(2) The intelligence community (IC) is responsible for providing adversary EOB data as well as sensor data on the EME to JEMSMO personnel in order to characterize the EMOE. JEMSMO personnel continually analyze the EMOE to provide feedback to the IC on the prioritization of EMS-related intelligence efforts.

(3) A wide range of national, theater, and component intelligence and communication systems is available to a JFC. The existence of this capability does not, however, ensure that intelligence and communications systems can be deployed without significant planning and coordination. The subordinate joint force intelligence directorate of a joint staff (J-2) must effectively coordinate communications architecture requirements with the communications system directorate of a joint staff (J-6).

For more information on intelligence communications requirements, refer to JP 2-01, Joint and National Intelligence Support to Military Operations.

CHAPTER II
INTERNATIONAL ELECTROMAGNETIC SPECTRUM MANAGEMENT

1. Introduction

a. All nations share the EMS and reserve their sovereign right to its unlimited use. At the international and national levels, the primary concern for the use of the EMS is economic and not military. International telecommunications cooperation is vital to support trade, transportation, communications, and mutual protection against interference. This chapter provides an overview of international, national, joint, and Service organizations and agencies that are primarily responsible for policy concerning spectrum use. Since both operational and tactical spectrum operations policy and decisions are based on international and national policy, it is important to understand the organizations and processes involved in spectrum operations at this level. The function of the Department of Defense (DOD) and Service-level EMS organizations is to provide regulatory guidance to the JFC in regards to lawful operation within the EMOE while satisfying operational demands. Finally, it is important for commanders to understand Service perspectives in order to fully benefit from integrated JEMSO functions.

b. All nations have a sovereign right to allocate the EMS as needed to support their national interests, but the successful conduct of operations requires the JFC to work with the nation at issue to balance these rights with the need to maintain security of US and multinational forces. The JFC and staff need to understand the national spectrum allocations for the country where the operation is taking place. Almost always this allocation will differ from US allocations, and US military systems could conflict with civilian use of the spectrum.

2. International Telecommunications Union

To promote international telecommunications cooperation to support trade, transportation, communications, and mutual protection against interference, most countries have agreed to generally follow International Telecommunications Union (ITU) Allocations, Standards and Radio Regulations for spectrum use. The ITU allocations for civil and military EMS use in North and South America are different than those used in the Middle East and Asia. Having a good understanding of the ITU and HN allocations for the joint operational area enhances the joint task force (JTF) staff's ability to prevent spectrum-use conflicts that could have a negative effect on military operations or civilian infrastructure.

3. Allied Electromagnetic Spectrum Management Authorities

When joint operations are conducted by an Allied force, it is necessary to understand SM roles, responsibilities, and processes within the alliance. These alliances are either long-standing relationships or ad hoc. The US is a member of two long-standing organizations: The North Atlantic Treaty Organization (NATO) and the Combined Communications–Electronics Board (CCEB).

a. **North Atlantic Treaty Organization.** NATO is a political and military alliance of 26 European and two North American nations. NATO organizations that have a role in EMS management operations are:

(1) Military Committee (MC) is the senior military authority in NATO, providing NATO's civilian decision-making bodies—the North Atlantic Council, the Defense Planning Committee, and the Nuclear Planning Group—with advice on military matters.

(2) The Civilian/Military Spectrum Capability Panel works directly for the MC on consultation, command, and control issues and is the sole competent source of advice and decisions on the management of the RF spectrum within NATO (see Figure II-1). It supports the MC and works with the strategic commands to satisfy NATO RF spectrum requirements

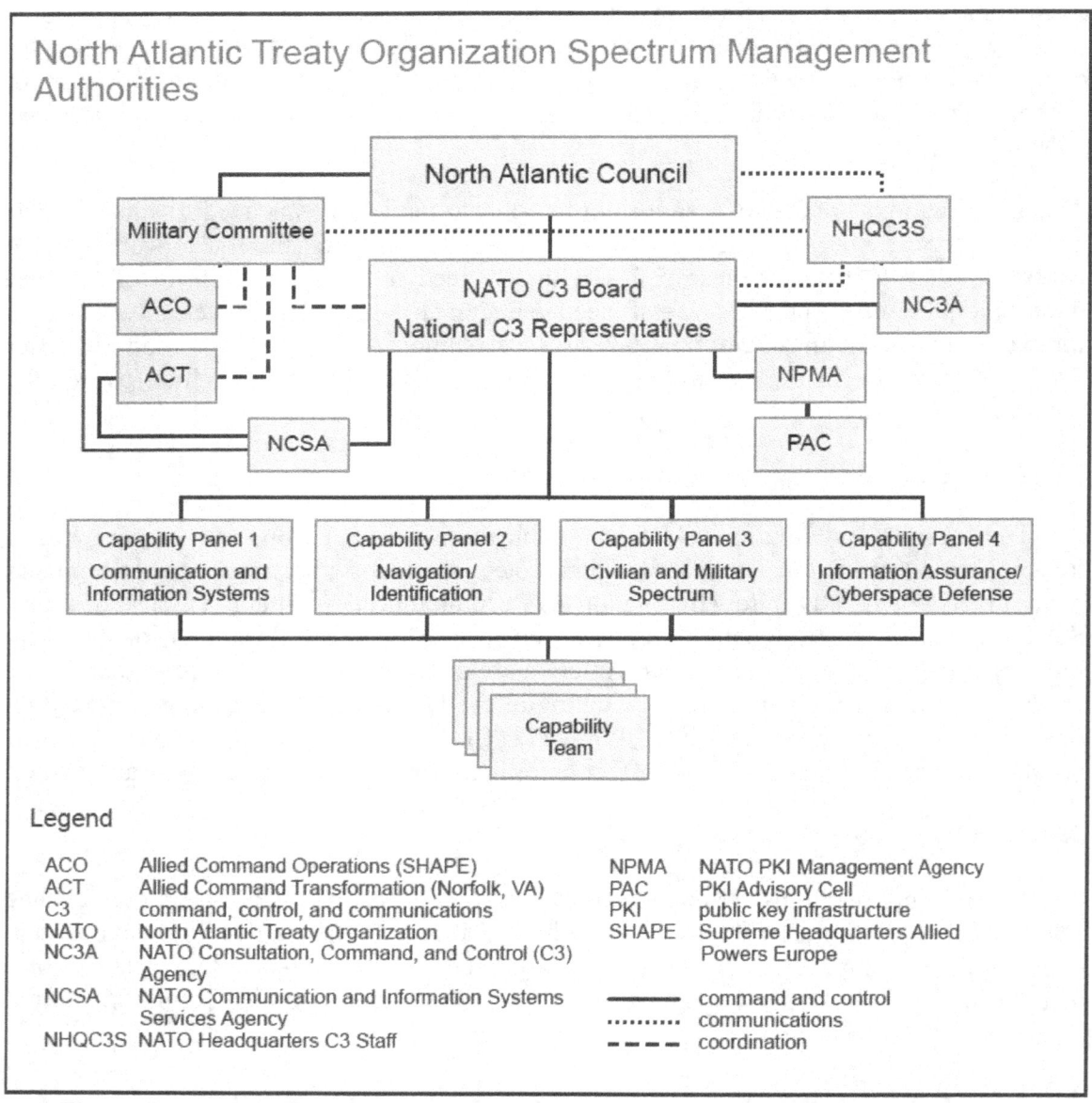

Figure II-1. North Atlantic Treaty Organization Spectrum Management Authorities

during peace, emergency, crisis, and wartime. The NATO Civilian/Military Spectrum Capability Panel is also responsible for maintaining the NATO supplements to Allied Communications Publication (ACP) 190, *Guide to Spectrum Management in Military Operations*.

(3) The Civilian/Military Spectrum Capability Panel is composed of representatives from the military and civil SM components of NATO member nations; the strategic commands; and the NATO Consultation, Command, and Control Agency (an acquisition and development organization). The Civilian/Military Spectrum Capability Panel also interacts with non-NATO nations in support of cooperative efforts involving frequency and SM issues. It may also deal with the military frequency and spectrum problems of other agencies/organizations, any separate NATO command that may be established later, or of the NATO nations (when called upon), provided this does not interfere with its primary mission.

(4) The NATO Headquarters Consultation, Command, and Control Staff Spectrum Management Branch (SMB) is the day-to-day staff charged with carrying out the necessary staff and operational work in support of the Civilian/Military Spectrum Capability Panel and the NATO nations and commands. Staff work includes diverse activities such as developing spectrum vision for NATO; developing and maintaining NATO spectrum policy and doctrine; providing advice to nations, organizations, and acquisition programs for spectrum-dependent equipment involving frequencies and spectrum; coordinating supportability assessments; management of the NATO portions of the 225–400 MHz band; and other tasks in support of the Civilian/Military Spectrum Capability Panel terms of reference (see the FM Handbook for more information).

(5) National Radio Frequency Agency. The SM office for the ministry of defense or chief of defense that acts as the national military frequency agency for a nation is usually called a national RF agency. This agency exists as the single interface for frequency and spectrum coordination and management issues between the Civilian/Military Spectrum Capability Panel SMB and the NATO nation on a national military level. See ACP 190(C), *Guide to Spectrum Management in Military Operations,* ACP190, NATO Supplement (SUPP)-1B, *NATO Guide to Spectrum Management in Military Operations, NATO Frequency Management Handbook,* and CCEB Publication 1, *Organization, Roles, Policies, and Responsibilities* for more information on Allied SM organizations.

b. **The Combined Communications–Electronics Board.** The CCEB is a five-nation, joint military communications–electronics (C-E) organization whose mission is the coordination of any military C-E matter that is referred to it by a member nation.

(1) The member nations of the CCEB are Australia, Canada, New Zealand, the United Kingdom, and the US.

(2) The CCEB has no standing forces so their focus is on interoperability between member nations. The CCEB principals consist of a senior communications representative from each of the member nations.

(3) The spectrum working group (WG) is the CCEB WG concerned with CCEB SM issues. Refer to CCEB Publication 1 for a full description of the organization and mission of the CCEB. Figure II-2 shows the current organizational structure of the CCEB.

(4) Historically, CCEB nations have had a major positive impact on NATO's wider allied communications (technical) interoperability through the generation and distribution of communications procedural documents titled ACPs. ACPs are issued as guidance for, and use by, allied forces of the nations represented on the CCEB and are appropriate for use in any theater or part of the world. The ACP base publications do not contain national or local theater, command, or geographically significant information. ACP supplements are provided to cover specific national, command, or geographic issues. Two key ACPs pertaining to SM are ACP 194, *Policy for the Coordination of Military Radio Frequency Allocations and Assignments Between Cooperating Nations,* and ACP 190, *Guide to Spectrum Management in Military Operations,* which has been supplemented by both the US and NATO.

4. Spectrum Support Outside the United States and Its Territories

a. There are very few standardized radio bands throughout the world, and to build a radio or system that will operate worldwide in a single band is not realistic. Systems procured by DOD must be designed to operate in a variety of bands to be of value,

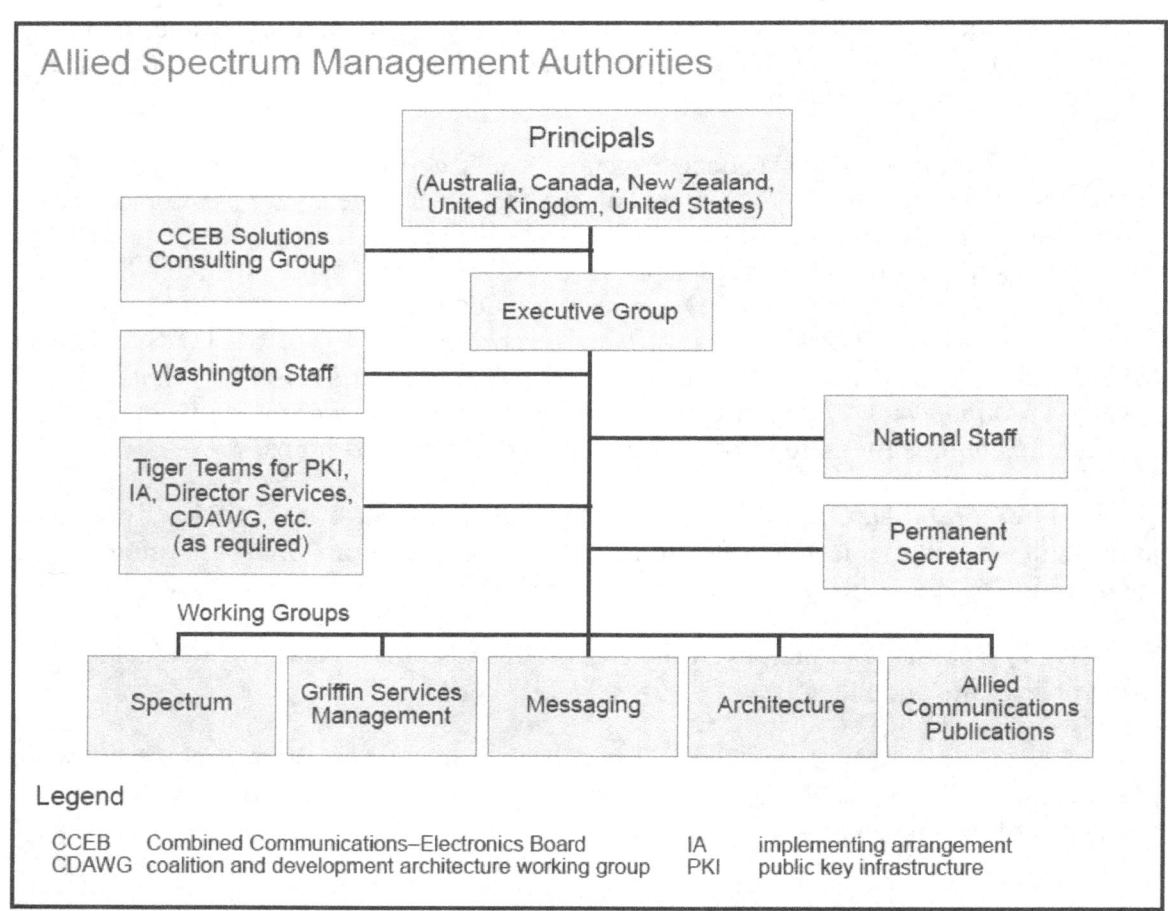

Figure II-2. Allied Spectrum Management Authorities

particularly to tactical operations. This is why multimode, multiband radios enjoy the greatest use among tactical operations.

b. The unified commanders, through the joint frequency management office (JFMO)/joint spectrum management element (JSME), will coordinate through the United States liaison office (USLO) or US office of military cooperation (OMC) to obtain spectrum support and negotiate frequency assignments from HM FM authorities to support military operations and exercises in their respective countries. To streamline the coordination process, the USLO or OMC may authorize direct coordination between the combatant command (CCMD) JFMO or JTF JSME and the HN FM authorities. Because it may be easier to include spectrum use in other agreements, the JFC may want to include RF spectrum access by US military forces in agreements such as:

(1) Status-of-forces agreements (SOFAs).

(2) HN security agreements with US forces.

(3) Protection of HN political, military, economic, social, information, and infrastructure considerations.

(4) Military and civil aviation agreements.

(5) JTF support agreements with the HN, other government departments and agencies, and nongovernmental organizations (NGOs), either directly or through the Department of State.

c. The JTF staff must ensure the JTF commander understands the impact of these agreements on the force's ability to conduct the mission. Any agreement that addresses spectrum access should include provisions for joint forces to utilize the RF spectrum for self-protection.

d. The JFC or JTF personnel shall neither initiate nor conduct the negotiation of an international agreement without the prior written approval by the DOD official (Chairman of the Joint Chiefs of Staff, CCDR, etc.), who has been assigned responsibility for agreements concerning spectrum management, access, and use.

5. International and Host Nation Laws and Regulations

Generally, an HN is any sovereign nation in which DOD plans or is likely to conduct military operations with the permission of that nation. Most nations have a single agency responsible for SM, normally the ministry of communications or some similar agency. In nations where DOD has established posts, camps, bases, or stations, there will normally be a liaison with the ministry established through which the EMSM will negotiate for spectrum support. As discussed previously, frequency allocations vary according to ITU region. Failure to adhere to these policies and guidance can result in monetary fines, equipment confiscation, and/or imprisonment, as well as possible mission failure, equipment damage, and loss of life.

CHAPTER III
NATIONAL DEFENSE ELECTROMAGNETIC SPECTRUM MANAGEMENT

1. National Electromagnetic Spectrum Authorities—Strategic Planning and Management of the Electromagnetic Spectrum

The Communications Act of 1934, as amended, governs radio EMS use in the US and its territories (see Figure III-1). The act established duality in SM in the US between the President for federal government stations and the Federal Communications Commission (FCC). The FCC regulates the spectrum use of non-federal operated radio stations, common carriers, and private organizations or individuals. By Executive Order 12016 of 1978, the President delegated his functions under the act to a new organization created as the National Telecommunications and Information Administration (NTIA) and placed them under the Secretary of Commerce.

a. **National Telecommunications and Information Administration.** The Communications Act of 1934 gave control of government radio stations to the President. The President, through the NTIA, will control all frequency resources in the US and its territories and will authorize foreign governments to construct and operate fixed service

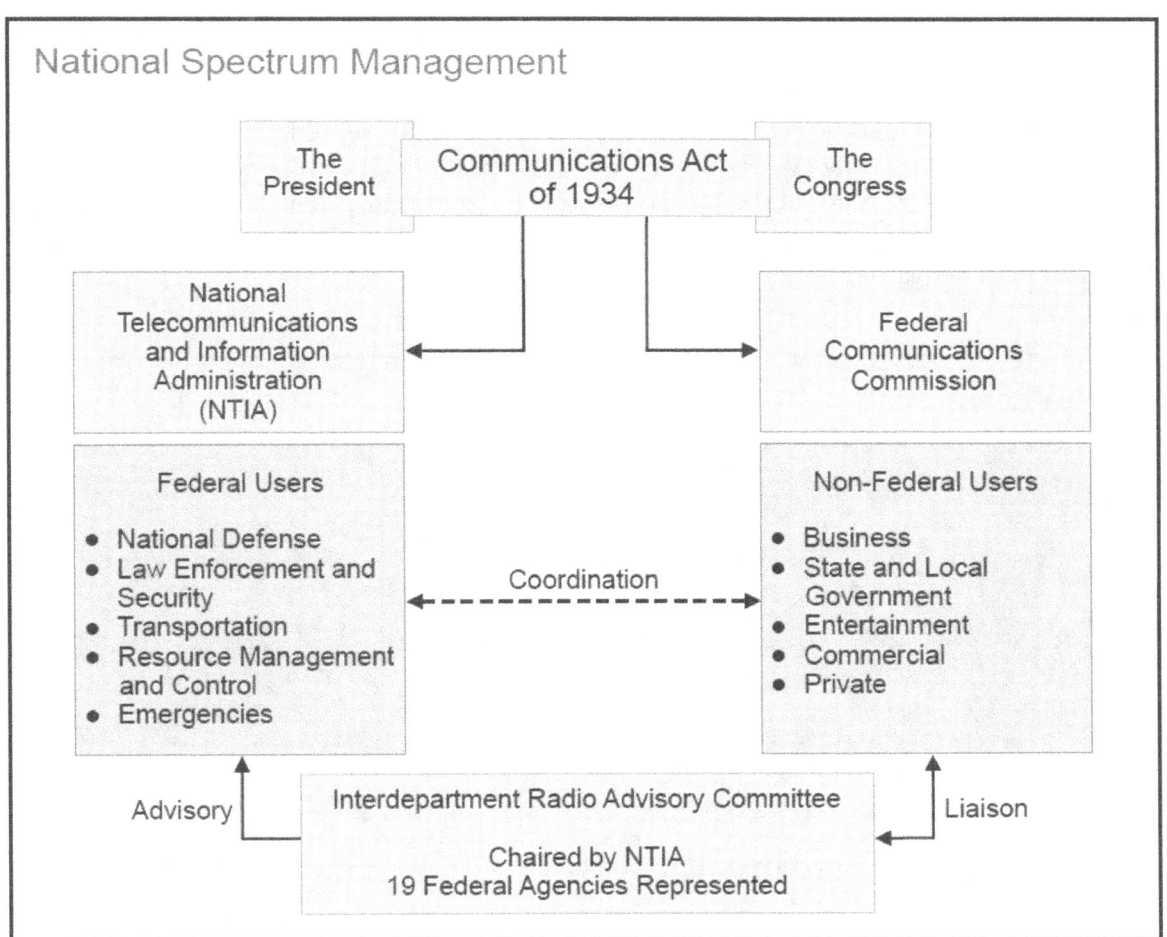

Figure III-1. National Spectrum Management

radio stations at their embassies. Frequencies are assigned to these stations if it is in the national interest and if foreign governments grant reciprocal privileges to the US. Figure III-2 illustrates the organization of the NTIA.

(1) **The Office of Spectrum Management (OSM).** The OSM formulates and establishes plans and policies that ensure the effective, efficient, and equitable use of the spectrum both nationally and internationally. Through the development of long-range spectrum plans, the OSM is prepared to address future US Government (USG) spectrum requirements, including public safety operations and the coordination and registration of USG satellite networks. The OSM also satisfies the frequency assignment needs of federal agencies and provides spectrum certification for new federal agency radio communication systems.

(2) **The Interdepartment Radio Advisory Committee (IRAC).** The IRAC, under the OSM, assists the NTIA Assistant Secretary in assigning frequencies to USG radio stations and in developing and executing policies, programs, procedures, and technical criteria pertaining to the allocation, management, and use of the spectrum. The IRAC consists of a main committee, six subcommittees, and several ad hoc WGs that consider various aspects of SM policy. The six current subcommittees are:

(a) Frequency Assignment Subcommittee (FAS). Responsible for functions related to the assignment and coordination of radio frequencies and the development and execution of procedures. The aeronautical assignment group (AAG) subgroup of the FAS is responsible for engineering the AAG frequency assignments and determining whether or not application for frequency assignment action in the AAG bands should be approved by NTIA. The AAG is chaired by the Federal Aviation Administration. The military assignment group (MAG) subgroup of the FAS is responsible for determining whether applications for frequency assignment in the MAG bands should be approved by NTIA. The MAG is chaired by the United States Air Force (USAF).

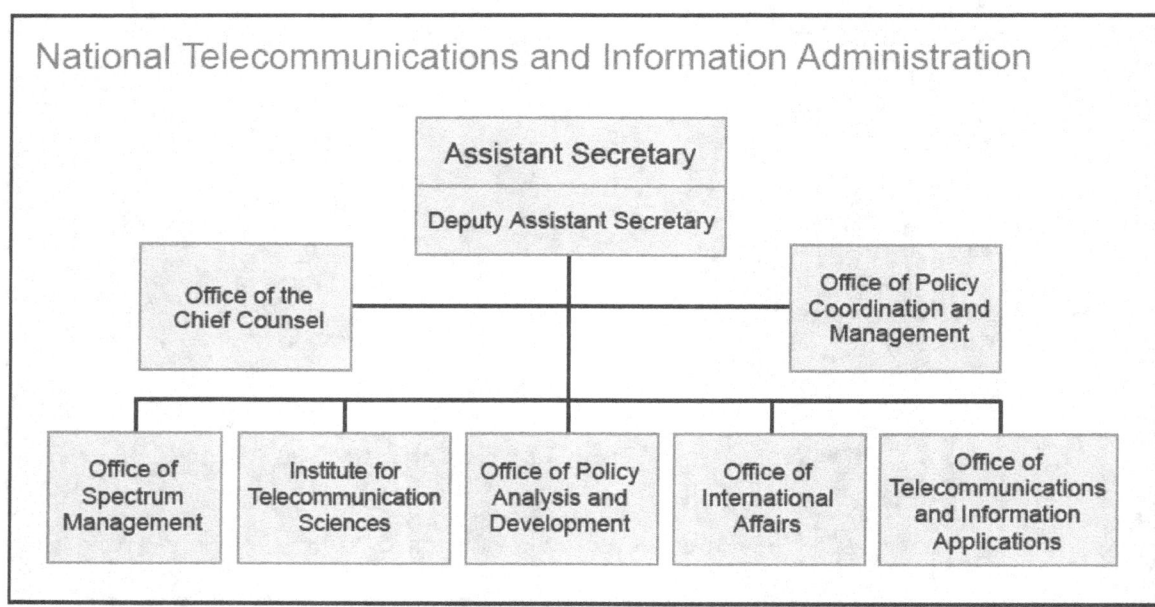

Figure III-2. National Telecommunications and Information Administration

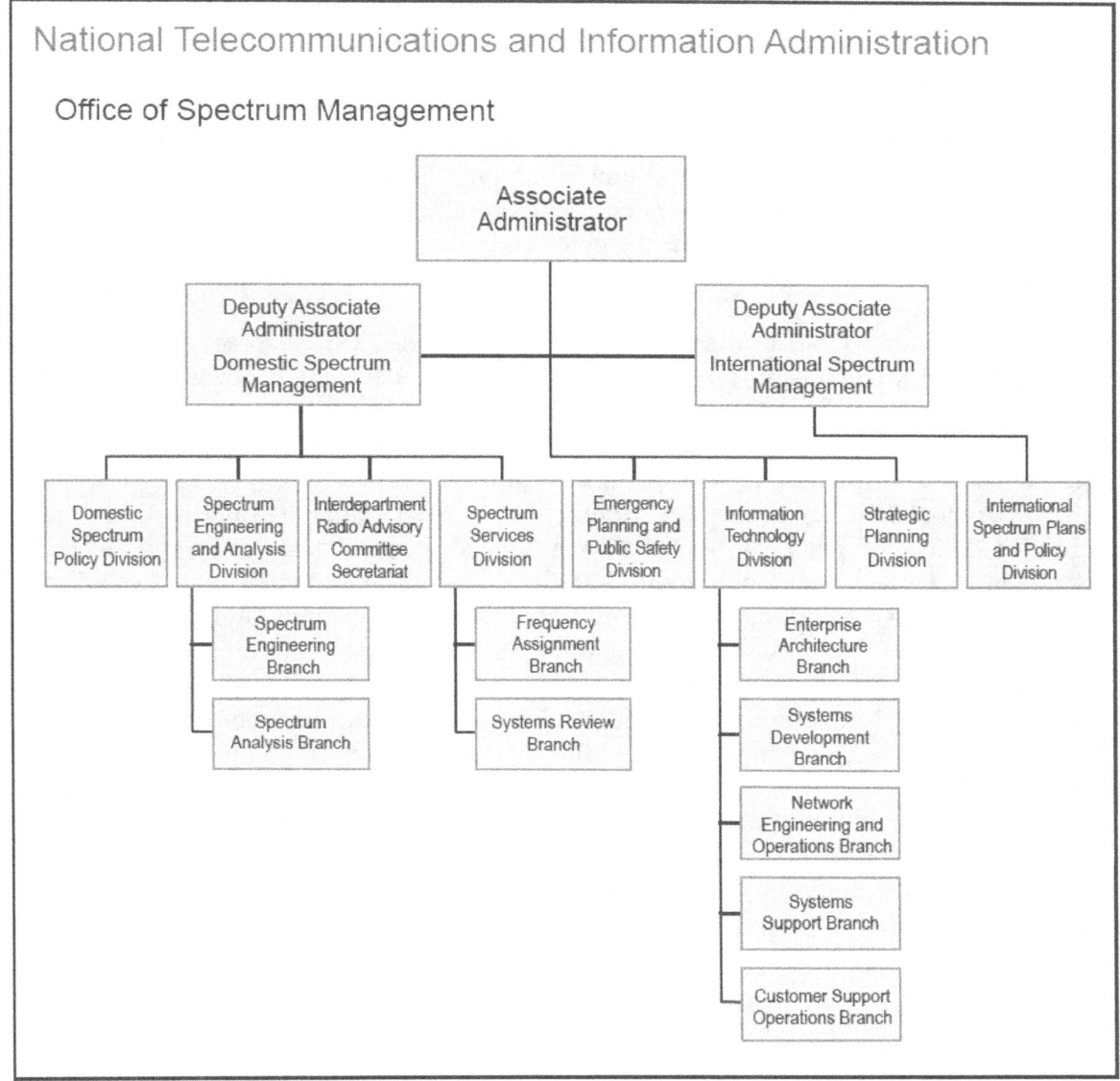

Figure III-2. National Telecommunications and Information Administration (continued)

(b) Spectrum Planning Subcommittee. Responsible for functions related to planning for the use of the EMS in the national interest to include the apportionment of spectrum space between or among the government and nongovernment activities and other such matters as the IRAC may direct.

(c) Technical Subcommittee. Develops recommended new standards and improvements of existing standards to optimize the use of the radio spectrum in the form of technical reports.

(d) Radio Conference Subcommittee. Responsible for functions that relate to preparing for ITU radio conferences, including the development of recommended US proposals and positions.

(e) Space Systems Subcommittee. Review, modify, develop, and maintain the procedures for the national implementation of the space related provisions of the ITU radio regulations.

(f) Emergency Planning Subcommittee. Formulate, guide, and review national security emergency preparedness planning for spectrum-dependent systems. From time to time, these subcommittees are reorganized, dissolved, created, or renamed. For more information about the IRAC and these subcommittees, see the NTIA Web site at http://www.ntia.doc.gov.

b. **The Federal Communications Commission.** The FCC is an independent federal regulatory agency responsible directly to Congress. It regulates interstate and international communications by radio, TV, wire, satellite, and cable in all 50 states, the District of Columbia, and US territories. The FCC is directed by five commissioners appointed by the President and confirmed by the Senate for 5-year terms, except when filling an unexpired term. The President designates one commissioner to serve as chairman. As the chief executive officer of the FCC, the chairman delegates management and administrative responsibility to the managing director. Certain other functions are delegated to staff units and bureaus and to committees of commissioners. The commissioners hold regular open and closed agenda meetings and special meetings. They also may act between meetings by "circulation," a procedure by which a document is submitted to each commissioner individually for consideration and official action. The FCC staff is organized by function. There are six operating bureaus and 10 staff offices. The bureaus' responsibilities include processing applications for licenses and other filings, analyzing complaints, conducting investigations, developing and implementing regulatory programs, and taking part in hearings. The offices provide support services. Even though the bureaus and offices have their individual functions, they regularly share expertise in addressing FCC issues. More on the FCC organizational structure and the bureaus and office functions are described on the FCC Web site (www.fcc.gov).

2. National Spectrum Supportability

a. Commanders must be aware of the policy and processes for national spectrum supportability. This is especially important because critical events occurring within the homeland, such as weapons of mass destruction events or natural disasters, require the coordination of civil and federal local, state, and national authorities whose equipment may operate, by law, in different frequency bands. This difference in frequency band usage is because, within the US and its territories, commanders must comply with the statutory EMS management requirements of the NTIA for federal systems and FCC regulations for civil systems. Both the National Guard Bureau (NGB) and the United States Coast Guard (USCG) may operate both civil and federal systems dependent upon the role they are assuming in operations (i.e., Title 10, United States Code [USC], versus Title 32, USC, or Title 14, USC, statuses.

b. Spectrum supportability is addressed in both regulation and policy, but it is important for commanders to have an overview of what the process is and how it is implemented so compliance can be maintained. The US Military Communications–Electronics Board

(MCEB) provides spectrum support guidance to DOD. This guidance outlines the general considerations, provisions, and restrictions that apply to a particular system concerning the use of the EMS. It is directive upon the submitting Service command, direct reporting unit or center, and the conditions of frequency assignment to the operational user.

c. The goal of the equipment spectrum certification process is to facilitate the timely provision of technical characteristics to determine compatibility and interoperability of systems that use the EMS in support of national needs and coalition missions and to derive whether these systems will operate in accordance with (IAW) the DOD, national, and international technical standards, rules, and regulations of SM. It is the responsibility of the milestone decision authority or component acquisition executive to ensure equipment is spectrum certified. The overall goal and intent is to assess the operational frequency supportability and EM compatibility in the intended environment. The process and procedures closely track the current acquisition process. The process provides support from early in the technology development phase (experimental) through the deployment and production phase and includes commercial and nondevelopmental items. Close coordination among operations, SM, and procurement personnel ensures effective/efficient use of the spectrum for peacetime and wartime operations. It is important for commanders to understand that there is a relationship between phases, acquisition categories, program milestone events, and the time required to gain approval for frequencies.

See Manual of Regulations and Procedures for Federal Radio Frequency Management (Redbook), *and ACP 190 US SUPP-1(D),* Guide to Frequency Planning, *for more information on spectrum supportability.*

3. Department of Defense Spectrum Authorities

This section describes the functions, relationship, and responsibilities of DOD SM organizations. For more information concerning DOD SM, see Department of Defense Instruction (DODI) 4650.01, *Policy and Procedures for Management and Use of the Electromagnetic Spectrum.*

a. SM within DOD is a cooperative process that is divided into three elements. The Office of the Assistant Secretary of Defense (Networks and Information Integration/Chief Information Officer) (OASD[NII/CIO]) is responsible for carrying out the policy, planning, and oversight functions associated with DOD spectrum matters. The Defense Spectrum Organization (DSO), which reports to the Defense Information Systems Agency (DISA), is responsible for providing the resources to coordinate joint spectrum matters and assists OASD(NII/CIO) in strategic spectrum planning. The SM offices of the Services manage the spectrum for their respective Services and interact with both civil and military agencies to coordinate joint issues. Figure III-3 shows the relationships of these organizations.

b. **The Office of the Assistant Secretary of Defense for Networks and Information Integration.** The Assistant Secretary for Defense for Networks and Information Integration is the chief information officer (CIO) for the DOD. The secretary serves as the principal staff assistant and advisor to the Secretary and Deputy Secretary of Defense on spectrum

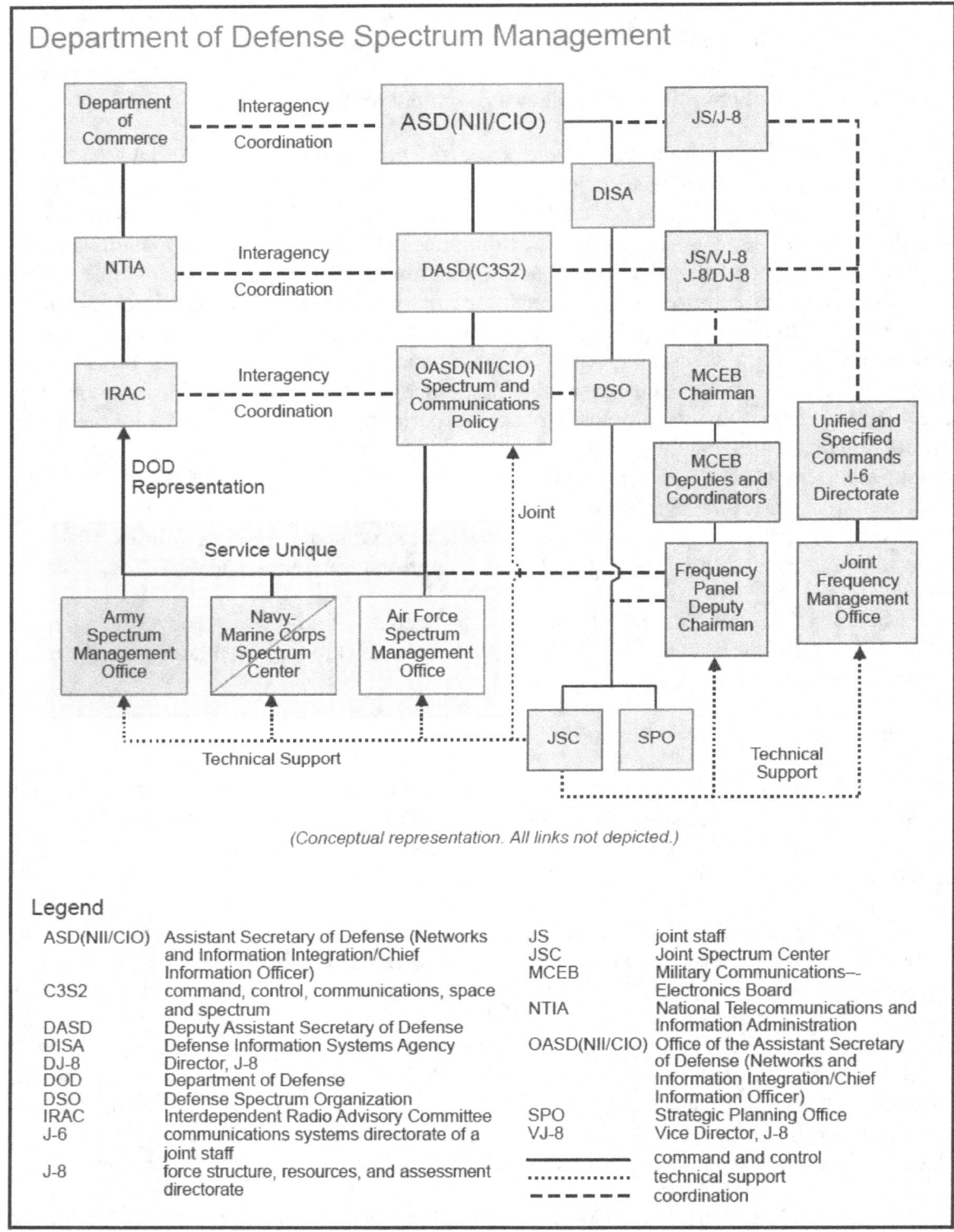

Figure III-3. Department of Defense Spectrum Management

related matters. Within the OASD(NII/CIO), the director of spectrum and communications policy provides day-to-day policy oversight and guidance to the DOD SM community.

c. United States Military Communications–Electronics Board

(1) The US MCEB is the principal DOD coordinating agency for SM. The MCEB functions under the policies and directives of the Secretary of Defense and the Joint Chiefs of Staff. The MCEB guides the DOD in preparing and coordinating technical directives and agreements and in allocating spectrum allotments from the NTIA. Its mission is three-fold: coordinate between DOD components, between DOD and other government departments and agencies, and between DOD and foreign nations.

(2) Membership of the MCEB is composed of the Director of Joint Staff, Joint Staff J-8, Deputy Director, Command, Control, Communications, and Computer Systems, (who also serves as chairman), representatives of each Service, USCG, DISA, Defense Intelligence Agency (DIA), National Security Agency, and the Assistant Deputy Director for Communications and Networks, who represents the CCDRs. Other DOD elements may participate when appropriate.

(3) The majority of DOD operational spectrum issues are processed through the Joint Frequency Panel (JFP) of the MCEB. The JFP consists of experts drawn from the components that are represented on the MCEB. The JFP reviews, develops, coordinates, and implements DOD directives, studies, reports, and recommendations for the MCEB. Specific spectrum issues are addressed by permanent WGs.

4. Defense Spectrum Organization

a. DSO is the DOD's center of excellence for preserving and enhancing access to spectrum resources. DSO supports a full range of initiatives and activities, ranging from long-term planning and development of advanced SM technologies to on-site problem solving for warfighters in the field. DSO's facilities and elements include the Joint Spectrum Center (JSC), the Strategic Planning Office, the Business Management Office, and the Program Management Office for the Global Electromagnetic Spectrum Information System. Figure III-3 shows the organizational structure of DSO and its relationships to other DOD SM organizations.

b. DSO engages in the full range of activities needed to support spectrum access for the DOD. It provides direct operational support to the Chairman of the Joint Chiefs of Staff, CCMDs, Secretaries of Military Departments (MILDEPs), and directors of DOD agencies to achieve national security and military objectives. DSO has leading experts in the areas of E3, information systems, SM, training, modeling, and simulation. It applies EM environmental databases and analysis tools to assist in both the acquisition and operation of DOD C-E assets. It provides services such as spectrum-planning guidance, system integration, system vulnerability analysis, environmental analysis, test and measurement support, and SM software development.

c. In addition, DSO supports the OASD(NII/CIO) on national and international spectrum issues and spectrum coordination. DSO leads SM transformation efforts to support future net-centric operations and warfare. It develops comprehensive and integrated spectrum planning and policy strategies for DOD and participates in international organizations that have SM responsibilities (e.g., ITU and NATO). DSO also develops working partnerships with other government departments and agencies, industry, and academia, and monitors and analyzes emerging spectrum technologies in order to incorporate optimal technology to meet DOD mission requirements.

d. The Joint Spectrum Center

(1) The JSC is a field office within DSO, has leading experts in the areas of spectrum planning, E3, information systems, modeling and simulation, and operations to provide complete, spectrum-related services to the MILDEPs and CCMDs. JSC has extensive experience in applying EM environmental databases and analysis tools to assist in both the acquisition and operation of C-E assets. JSC is a source of engineering expertise and services dedicated to ensuring effective use of the EMS. JSC provides services such as spectrum-planning guidance, system integration, system vulnerability analysis, environmental analysis, test and measurement support, operational support, and SM software development.

(2) JSC provides support for spectrum planning, spectrum certification of new weapon and sensor system development, and training and operational support to the unified commands, MILDEPs, and DOD agencies. These services are also available to federal and local government activities. Additionally, foreign nations can obtain assistance through foreign military sales channels. JSC can provide these services to US industries when the efforts are determined to be in the interest of national security. For more information and details on JSC services, visit http://www.disa.mil/jsc/index.htm.

5. **Combatant Commander Spectrum Offices**

a. **Joint Frequency Management Office**

(1) Each GCC is specifically tasked by Chairman of the Joint Chiefs of Staff Instruction (CJCSI) 3320.01C, *Electromagnetic Spectrum Use in Joint Military Operations*, to establish an FM structure that includes a JFMO and to establish procedures to support planned and ongoing operations. The supported GCC authorizes and controls use of the spectrum resources by the military forces under his or her command.

(2) Each supported GCC establishes a command policy on how the spectrum is used in his or her area of responsibility (AOR), obtains clearance (or approval) from HNs for use of the spectrum (through existing coordination procedures), and ensures that assigned military forces are authorized sufficient use of the spectrum to execute their designated missions. To accomplish these tasks, each supported GCC establishes a JFMO (see Figure III-4), typically under the cognizance of the J-6, to support joint planning, coordination, and control of the spectrum for assigned forces.

b. **Joint Spectrum Management Element.** At the JTF level, a JSME may be established. The JSME within a JTF may be assigned from the J-6 staff, from a component's staff, or from an external command. The JSME within a JTF must be staffed with trained EMSMs, preferably with experience in joint spectrum use and knowledge of the spectrum requirements of the CCMD's component forces. The process outlined above for the JFMO

Joint Frequency Management Office Spectrum
Management Process

1   Develops the spectrum-use plan using system data contained in the JOPES. This is particularly vital in support of command and control hand-overs that are highly dependent on spectrum-dependent systems.

2   In conjunction with the J-2, J-3, and J-6, prepares a JRFL for approval by the J-3 (through the electronic warfare cell or equivalent).

3   Periodically updates and distributes the JRFL, as necessitated by changes in the task organization, geography, and joint communications-electronics operation instructions and by transition through operational phases.

4   Provides administrative and technical support for military spectrum use.

5   Exercises frequency allotment and assignment authority. This may be delegated to facilitate decentralization and to provide components with the maximum latitude and flexibility in support of combat operations.

6   Establishes and maintains the common database necessary for planning, coordinating, and controlling spectrum use. This database should contain spectrum-use information on all emitters and receivers (critical, friendly, military and civilian, available enemy, and neutral) as appropriate for the area of responsibility involved.

7   Analyzes and evaluates potential spectrum-use conflicts.

8   In accordance with J-5 guidance, coordinates military spectrum use with the spectrum authorities of the United Nations or host nations involved.

9   Serves as the focal point for inclusion of spectrum-use considerations in the JOPES.

10   Receives, reports on, analyzes, and attempts to resolve incidents of unacceptable electromagnetic interference; refers incidents that cannot be resolved to the next higher spectrum management authority.

Legend

J-2	intelligence directorate of a joint staff	J-6	communications system directorate of a joint staff
J-3	operations directorate of a joint staff	JOPES	Joint Operation Planning and Execution System
J-5	plans directorate of a joint staff	JRFL	joint restricted frequency list

Figure III-4. Joint Frequency Management Office Spectrum Management Process

will be mirrored by the JSME at the JTF level. Chairman of the Joint Chiefs of Staff Manual (CJCSM) 3320.01B, *Joint Operations in the Electromagnetic Battlespace*, provides additional information about JFMO/JSME functions and processes.

6. Service Spectrum Management Authorities

a. **Air Force.** The Air Force Spectrum Management Office (AFSMO) mission is to plan, provide, and preserve access to the EMS for the Air Force and selected DOD activities. AFSMO does this in support of national policy objectives, systems development, and global operations through analysis and negotiation with international and national civil and military organizations. AFSMO is composed of two directorates. The Directorate of Operations is responsible for day-to-day spectrum processes that allow Air Force and DOD warfighters unfettered access to the EMS worldwide. The key operations processes are obtaining spectrum certification for new equipment, similar to a building permit, and frequency assignments, or the legal authorization to operate that equipment in the US. The Directorate of Strategic Planning is the Air Force voice in international, national, civil, and military (NATO and multinational) EMS forums and is responsible for the development of integrated spectrum plans and long-term strategies to address current and future needs for Air Force spectrum access. AFSMO also provides curriculum oversight for the Electromagnetic Spectrum Management Course and the Joint Task Force Spectrum Management Course.

For more information on Air Force SM, refer to Air Force Instruction (AFI) 33-118, Electromagnetic Spectrum Management.

b. **Army**

(1) The Army Spectrum Management Office (ASMO) is the Army Service-level office for all spectrum-related matters. The ASMO coordinates RF spectrum policy and guidance and represents the Army in spectrum negotiations with civil, military, national, and international regulatory organizations. The Army Spectrum Manager (ASM) directs Army-wide SM activities, develops and implements SM policy, and allocates frequency resources (frequency assignment) to support the Army. The ASM serves as the principal advisor to the Army CIO/ signal staff officer (G-6) in regard to RF SM and radio regulatory matters.

(2) The Army Frequency Management Office–Continental United States (AFMO-CONUS) is the Army's principal field office providing SM support for all unit, installation, and special case Army customers requiring tactical, non-tactical, communications and non-communications frequencies. For the continental United States (CONUS)-related matters, this is the tactical EMSM's primary resource. CONUS is broken down by region and assigned an area frequency coordinator.

c. **Marine Corps.** The Director, C4, Headquarters, Marine Corps (HQMC C4)/Department of the Navy (DON) Deputy CIO Marine Corps, provides Marine Corps EMS policy and oversees spectrum use, requirements, and operations. HQMC C4 establishes Marine Corps policy; provides oversight, guidance, and procedures relating to the proper and efficient management of the EMS; provides Marine Corps representation (at the policy level) to various national, DOD, joint, and DON organizations, WGs, and forums; and provides administrative, technical, and operational support to the operating forces and supporting establishment in support of Marine Corps EMS operational requirements. Marine Corps management and use of the EMS are governed IAW Marine Corps Order (MCO) 2400.2, *Marine Corps Management and Use of the Electromagnetic Spectrum.*

d. **Navy and Marine Corps**

(1) The Navy and Marine Corps Spectrum Center (NMSC) coordinates SM policy and guidance and represents the Navy, and when required, the Marine Corps, in spectrum negotiations with civil, military, and national regulatory organizations. The NMSC coordinates spectrum certification actions for Navy and Marine Corps systems/equipments. In addition, the NMSC coordinates, registers, assigns, and protects radio frequencies for test, evaluation, and operational use of spectrum-dependent equipment and systems by all Navy and Marine Corps activities in the US and territories.

(2) The Navy and Marine Corps spectrum offices (NMCSOs) are the Navy's principal regional offices providing administrative SM support and assistance for all unit, installation, and Navy customers requiring tactical, non-tactical, communications and non-communications frequency assignment requests for the US and its territories. Outside CONUS, EMS support must follow CCMD guidance.

For more information on Navy and Marine Corps spectrum management, refer to Naval Telecommunications Procedures 6, Navy Electromagnetic Spectrum (EMS) Guide, *Chief of Naval Operations Instruction 2400.20F,* Electromagnetic Environmental Effects (E3) and Spectrum Supportability Policy and Procedures, *and MCO 2400.2* Marine Corps Management and Use of the Electromagnetic Spectrum.

e. **Coast Guard.** The USCG Spectrum Management and Telecommunications Policy Division, COMMANDANT (CG-652) Office is the USCG Service-level office for all spectrum-related matters. USCG, CG-652, falls under the Deputy Commandant for Mission Support. The Spectrum Management and Telecommunications Policy Division (CG-652) manages RF spectrum policy and guidance and represents the USCG in the coordination of SM issues with civil, military, national, and international regulatory organizations. CG-652 directs USCG-wide SM activities, develops and implements SM policies, and allocates frequency resources (i.e., frequency assignments) to support the USCG missions: maritime safety (marine safety and search and rescue); maritime security (drug and migrant interdiction, port waterways and coastal security); maritime stewardship (marine resources, environmental protection, aids to navigation, ice operations); and national defense and DOD interoperability. CG-652 serves as the principal advisor to the USCG CIO/CG-6 in regard to RF SM and frequency spectrum regulatory matters. The Spectrum Management Division has strategically placed principal EMSMs at district headquarters offices throughout the US. These individuals are the principal field office representatives providing SM support for all districts, units, installations, and special case USCG customers. USCG spectrum support is organized by districts and supported by field spectrum managers.

(1) **Commands.** Area and district commands are responsible for SM and frequency plans for units under their command. Area and district commands will validate spectrum requirements for units under their authority. Area and district commands are responsible for obtaining spectrum authority for spectrum-dependent equipment that is installed or maintained by the organization.

(2) **USCG Auxiliary.** The USCG Auxiliary serves as the civilian, nonmilitary component of the USCG. Auxiliarists provide direct operational and administrative support to many local USCG units. The USCG Auxiliary, when in direct support of USCG operations, will submit requests for frequency authority to the local sector/district commander for validation and further processing through CG-652. The USCG Auxiliary, as an organization, must be operating in support of the USCG to obtain authorization from NTIA to transmit on radio frequencies.

f. **National Guard Bureau**

(1) The NGB J-6/C4 SMB is the designated office within NGB responsible for planning and executing SM for assigned forces and providing support to the National Guard (NG) joint force headquarters-state (JFHQ-State) in communications with United States Northern Command (USNORTHCOM). NGB J-6/C4 SMB provides spectrum support to NG forces in state active duty and Title 32, USC, status to facilitate coordination with USNORTHCOM and federal agencies on spectrum usage during homeland defense (HD) or defense support of civil authorities (DSCA) operations.

(2) NG JFHQ-state spectrum managers should ensure use of their assigned spectrum resources are IAW current procedures to ensure unity of effort with Title 10, USC, forces conducting domestic operations. JFC and staff should be aware that conducting operations in a state requires coordination with the NG JFHQ-state spectrum manager and state emergency operations center.

7. Installation Electromagnetic Spectrum Management

a. The commander of a military installation will normally have responsibility for spectrum operations on the installation. This includes equipment and systems that have both permanent and temporary assignments. The installation commander is responsible for all EM radiation emanating from the installation and their outlying activities while ensuring a viable RF management program is in place to support base requirements. The installation commander can prohibit any RF emitter from operating when there is anticipated interference to mission-essential EM equipment. The installation EMSM maintains a current listing or electronic database of all frequencies assigned to the installation and outlying activities hosted by the installation. The installation EMSM provides all installation units with generated site licenses of major command frequency assignment notifications for all frequencies used.

b. For installation SM operations, the installation commander should ensure that the EMSM is properly trained. Spectrum operations constitute dealing with international and national laws on a regular basis in addition to safety of life issues. Assigning this responsibility as an additional duty or temporary assignment could have severe repercussions.

c. Commanders should ensure equipment has the proper certification and clearance to operate, that users are provided clear guidance on the operation of spectrum-dependent systems, and that programs and processes are in place to plan, manage, and execute installation spectrum operations.

d. Commanders should also:

(1) Provide spectrum policy, guidance, and procedures for the effective and efficient management and use of the EMS.

(2) Ensure SM is considered at all levels of operational planning and establish processes and procedures for the planning, assignment, coordination, deconfliction, and utilization of the EMS.

(3) Ensure compliance with applicable international, national, DOD, joint, statutory, and regulatory policies, to include spectrum supportability, certification, and HNC, is validated/completed for spectrum-dependent equipment and systems prior to operational use.

(4) Coordinate administrative and operational SM support requirements in support of the JFC.

For Service specific guidance on EMS management on installations, see Army Regulation (AR) 5-12, Army Management of the Electromagnetic Spectrum, *Field Manual 6-02.70,* Army Electromagnetic Spectrum Operations, *MCO 2400.2,* Marine Corps Management and Use of the Electromagnetic Spectrum, *MCO 2410.2B,* Electromagnetic Environmental Effects (E3) Control Program, *and AFI 33-118,* Electromagnetic Spectrum Management.

CHAPTER IV
ORGANIZING FOR JOINT ELECTROMAGNETIC SPECTRUM OPERATIONS

1. Introduction

a. How joint forces are organized to plan and execute JEMSMO is a **prerogative of the JFC.** Many factors are considered that affect the size and organization of the commander's staff. These factors include the mission or missions the joint force is tasked to accomplish, and the time allocated to accomplish the mission or missions. This chapter discusses **nominal organizations and staff** functions to plan and execute JEMSMO in joint operations. This chapter also provides a high-level view of how the Services organize in relation to joint operations.

b. **Joint Electromagnetic Spectrum Operational Environment**

(1) The use of the EMS is essential to all operations at all levels of command. Few, if any, military operations conducted involve only one Service. In a joint environment, the Services often compete for use of the spectrum to accomplish their missions. Joint operations require precise coordination and establishment of operating procedures not only for military operations but for HN coordination in order to most effectively use this finite resource.

(2) Since military operations rely on capabilities, equipment, and systems using the limited resources of the EMS, requirements may exceed the amount of spectrum available. As a result, efficient use and control of the spectrum are critical to operational success.

(3) The rapid growth of sophisticated weapons systems, as well as networked operations and communications systems, greatly increases demand for frequencies. Lack of preplanned frequency coordination and consideration of E3 will have an adverse effect upon friendly but competing users. Spectrum availability is further constrained by commercial applications and the rights of sovereign nations to govern EMS use within a particular country's national borders.

(4) Joint and multinational operations must also consider the needs of multinational forces in future contingencies. An effective SM structure is required not only to satisfy spectrum needs of military users but also to coordinate with HNs to facilitate effective use of this finite resource.

2. Responsibilities

Outlined below are the responsibilities and duties, broken down by command echelon, as they apply to JEMSMO.

a. **Combatant Commander**

(1) It is the responsibility of the CCDR to establish and promulgate command-specific policy and guidance for EMS use, the JRFL process, the JCEOI, software defined

radio waveform implementation and sharing, and other processes or directives that uniquely apply to the area (e.g., radar restrictions).

(2) Other duties are to establish a standing FM structure that includes a JFMO and procedures to support planned and ongoing operations. Specific actions will be taken to:

(a) Ensure operational, contingency, and communications plans address coordination among forces using the spectrum to enable effective exchange of information, eliminate duplication of effort, and achieve mutual support.

(b) Ensure plans address any necessary augmentation of the JFMO and/or JSME to support the effort.

(c) Resolve user conflicts not resolved at a lower level.

(d) Maintain close contact with appropriate multinational forces to ensure that mutual spectrum support is considered in multinational planning, operations, training, and exercises.

(e) Function as controlling authority for the JCEOI.

(f) Function as controlling authority for spectrum policy, to include frequencies for software defined radios.

b. **JFMO.** There is no standard JFMO organizational structure. A JFMO is a permanent organization within the CCMD. Each GCC organizes the JFMO IAW geographic and functional requirements. Typically, the JFMO is staffed with a DOD civilian as the chief and action officers who are responsible for programs, planning, analysis, or geographic regions. A JFMO may range in size from five to 10 personnel and is usually a combination of civilians and Service members. Figure IV-1 depicts a notional JFMO. The responsibilities of the JFMO are to:

(1) Exercise CCMD echelon core functions of JEMSMO (SM, FM, JSIR, HNC).

(2) Maintain the common frequency database necessary for planning, coordinating, and controlling spectrum use. The frequency database should contain all communication and non-communication spectrum emitters and receivers. Examples of such emitters are radars, unmanned vehicles, and sensors.

(3) Participate as a member of the GCC's EWC.

(a) Combine J-2, J-3, and J-6 inputs to develop a proposed JRFL.

(b) Update and distribute the JRFL, as required. Assist and coordinate the resolution and deconfliction of spectrum conflicts.

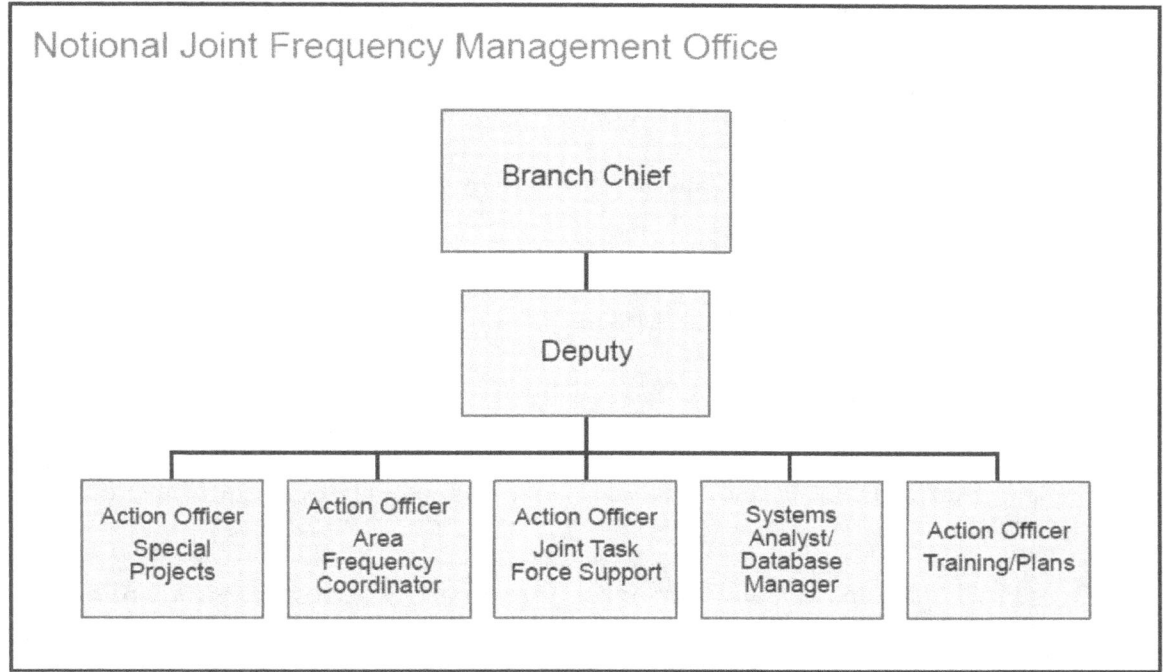

Figure IV-1. Notional Joint Frequency Management Office

(4) Perform HNC functions IAW plans directorate of a joint staff (J-5). HNC may involve the spectrum authority of the HN(s) involved, the US embassy defense attaché OMC, friendly forces coordination cell, etc.

(5) Be the focal point for inclusion of spectrum-use considerations in the communications annex of operation plans (OPLANs) and concept plans (CONPLANs).

(6) Perform JSIR functions IAW CJCSM 3320.02C, *Joint Spectrum Interference Resolution (JSIR) Procedures*. Develop and disseminate policy and procedures to handle EMI occurrences. Report, update, and track the status of all EMI occurrences using the JSIR Online collaboration portal. Monitor the JSIR Online collaboration portal for situational awareness and monitor classified e-mail for JSIR Online alerts. Assist and coordinate in the resolution of EMI occurrences as needed, to include terrestrial and space based systems.

(7) Perform the duties required to manage the JCEOI until the JTF J-6 is established.

NOTE: Within the bounds of proper classification and with the approval of the local commander, the finished JCEOI will be shared with interagency participants in a given operation.

(8) Provide guidance and procedures for post-conflict SM transitions.

(9) Coordinate, manage, and maintain frequencies for software-defined radios.

c. **Joint Force Commander.** The duties of the JFC are to:

(1) Follow established GCC EMS use policy and guidance, as required.

(2) Work with the CCMD's staff if modifications to the spectrum-use policy are necessary for specific situation(s).

(3) For operations outside of the GCC's AOR, assume the responsibilities listed for the commander.

(4) Coordinate with supporting CCDRs to determine what functions their staffs must undertake to control use of the EMS and what outside support is available.

(5) When directed, the JFC will establish a JSME to ensure that JTF forces are authorized sufficient use of the EMS to execute their assigned missions.

d. **JFC Staff.** The JTF and functional area cells of the JFC's staff have duties as follows:

(1) JTF Manpower and Personnel Directorate. Duties are to coordinate all personnel augmentation for the JSME and ensure the augmentees are added to the time-phased force and deployment data.

(2) JTF J-2. Duties are to:

(a) Participate (through the EWC) in spectrum-use conflict resolution.

(b) Assess intelligence needs and provide the J-6 with prioritized spectrum-use requirements for intelligence operations.

(c) Provide JRFL input.

(d) Provide the JSME with available enemy spectrum-use data IAW releasability constraints.

(e) Include spectrum-use requirements in the Joint Operation Planning and Execution System (JOPES).

(f) Assist the J-6 with JSIR.

(3) JTF J-3. Duties are to:

(a) Prioritize, for the JSME, all spectrum-use conflicts that occur.

(b) Provide spectrum-use requirements to J-6 for inclusion in the JOPES.

(c) Provide concept of operations (CONOPS).

(d) Comply with and enforce HERO, HERP, and HERF guidelines.

(e) Provide and validate JRFL inputs; approve consolidated JRFL.

(f) Prioritize systems when there is insufficient spectrum to support them all.

(4) EWC. Duties are to:

(a) Provide the JFC with effective EW planning and execution capability throughout all areas of operations.

(b) Assist the JSME in developing, compiling, and distributing the JRFL.

(c) Assist the component EWCs and JFC's J-6 in assessing instances of hostile EW and assist the JSME in assessing situations requiring EW deconfliction.

(d) Assist in the resolution of JSIRs and cases of EW-related EMI.

(5) JTF Logistics Directorate. Duties are to provide the JSME with any required spectrum-use considerations at ports of embarkation and debarkation, or waypoints during the deployment or redeployment phases.

(6) JTF J-5. Duties are to:

(a) Ensure SM is incorporated into long-range planning and future operations. Integrate inputs from the J-2, J-3, and J-6.

(b) Establish coordination channels, as required, to negotiate military spectrum use where procedures do not already exist.

(7) JTF J-6. Duties are to:

(a) Provide the JSME with the JTF nets to be included in the JCEOI.

(b) Assist in integrating EW activity into operations to minimize impact on friendly use of the EMOE.

(c) Update the JRFL as required.

(d) Assist the JSME with resolution of reported instances of interference or disruption.

(e) Provide JOPES data.

(8) Joint Communications Control Center (JCCC) Staff. The duties of the JCCC are to perform SM functions during joint operations and exercises.

(9) JSME. The duties of the JSME are to:

(a) Report all instances of interference IAW CJCSM 3320.02C, *Joint Spectrum Interference Resolution (JSIR) Procedures.*

(b) Establish JTF specific guidance for JEMSMO (SM, FM, JSIR, HNC) functions, to include the JRFL process, JCEOI, and other processes.

(c) Gather requirements from J-2, J-3, and J-6 to develop a JTF JRFL for approval by the J-3.

(d) Participate in the EWC representing SM issues.

(e) Exercise FM functions. Authority to issue frequency assignments or allotments may be delegated. However, the JSME must ensure that components with overlapping geographic areas are not allowed to make multiple frequency assignments on the same RF band.

(f) Report all incidents of EMI.

(g) Maintain the common spectrum-use database necessary for planning and coordinating access to the EMOE. This database contains spectrum-use information on all friendly, military and civilian, enemy, and neutral forces.

(h) Perform HNC functions as delegated by JFMO. HNC will be coordinated with the spectrum authority of the HN(s) or multinational forces involved IAW with J-5 guidance.

(i) Perform JSIR functions IAW CJCSM 3320.02C, *Joint Spectrum Interference Resolution (JSIR) Procedures.* Develop policy procedures and tracking status of EMI.

e. **Functional Component Commanders.** The duties of the functional component commanders are to:

(1) Provide component JCEOI input to include all call words requirements.

(2) Consolidate and validate component spectrum-use requirements.

(3) Provide component JRFL input.

f. **Service Component Commanders.** The duties of the Service component commanders are to:

(1) Consolidate and validate component spectrum-use requirements.

(2) Provide component JRFL input.

(3) Receive reports, identify, and attempt to resolve Service-specific EMI.

(4) Provide sufficient number of trained EMSMs.

g. **Spectrum Users.** The duties of the spectrum user are to:

(1) Obtain frequency authorization for each use of the EMS by their appropriate joint force component.

(2) Use frequencies as assigned and operate systems IAW parameters authorized by the frequency assignment process.

(3) Coordinate any need to exceed or operate spectrum-dependent equipment outside the parameters authorized by the appropriate spectrum-use plan.

(4) Ensure the spectrum-dependent equipment is properly maintained to preclude unintentional violation of authorized spectrum-use parameters.

3. Service Organizations

a. Air Force

(1) JEMSMO supports and enables all USAF warfighting functions. USAF JEMSMO assets are organized to ensure that JEMSMO are integral to the commander's overall CONOPS. At each echelon of USAF organization responsible for JEMSMO, the communications staff officer (A-6), in coordination with the intelligence staff officer (A-2) and operations staff officer (A-3), are responsible for planning and coordinating JEMSMO. The EMSM is responsible to the A-6 and coordinates directly with the A-2 and A-3 staffs for planning, coordinating, synchronizing, and deconflicting JEMSMO actions. Figure IV-2 depicts typical USAF coordination channels.

(2) USAF commanders support JEMSMO by having trained personnel well-versed in joint operations. Whether as the lead Service or supporting another Service's spectrum operations, USAF EMSMs must understand Service-unique spectrum planning, coordinating, and operating parameters to be an effective member of the team.

b. Army

(1) EMS operations support and enable all Army warfighting functions. Army EMS operations assets are organized to ensure that EMS operations are integral to the commander's overall CONOPS. At each echelon of Army organization responsible for electromagnetic spectrum management operations, the assistant chief of staff (ACOS), G-6, in coordination with the ACOS, intelligence staff officer (G-2), and ACOS, operations staff officer (G-3), is responsible for planning and coordinating EMS operations. The EMSM(s) is responsible to the G-6 and coordinates directly with the components of the G-2 and G-3 for planning, coordinating, synchronizing, and deconflicting EMS management operations' actions. Figure IV-3 depicts typical Army coordination channels.

(2) Army commanders support JEMSMO by having trained personnel well-versed in joint operations. Whether as the lead Service or supporting another Service's spectrum operations, Army EMSMs must understand Service-unique spectrum planning, coordinating, and operating parameters to be an effective member of the team.

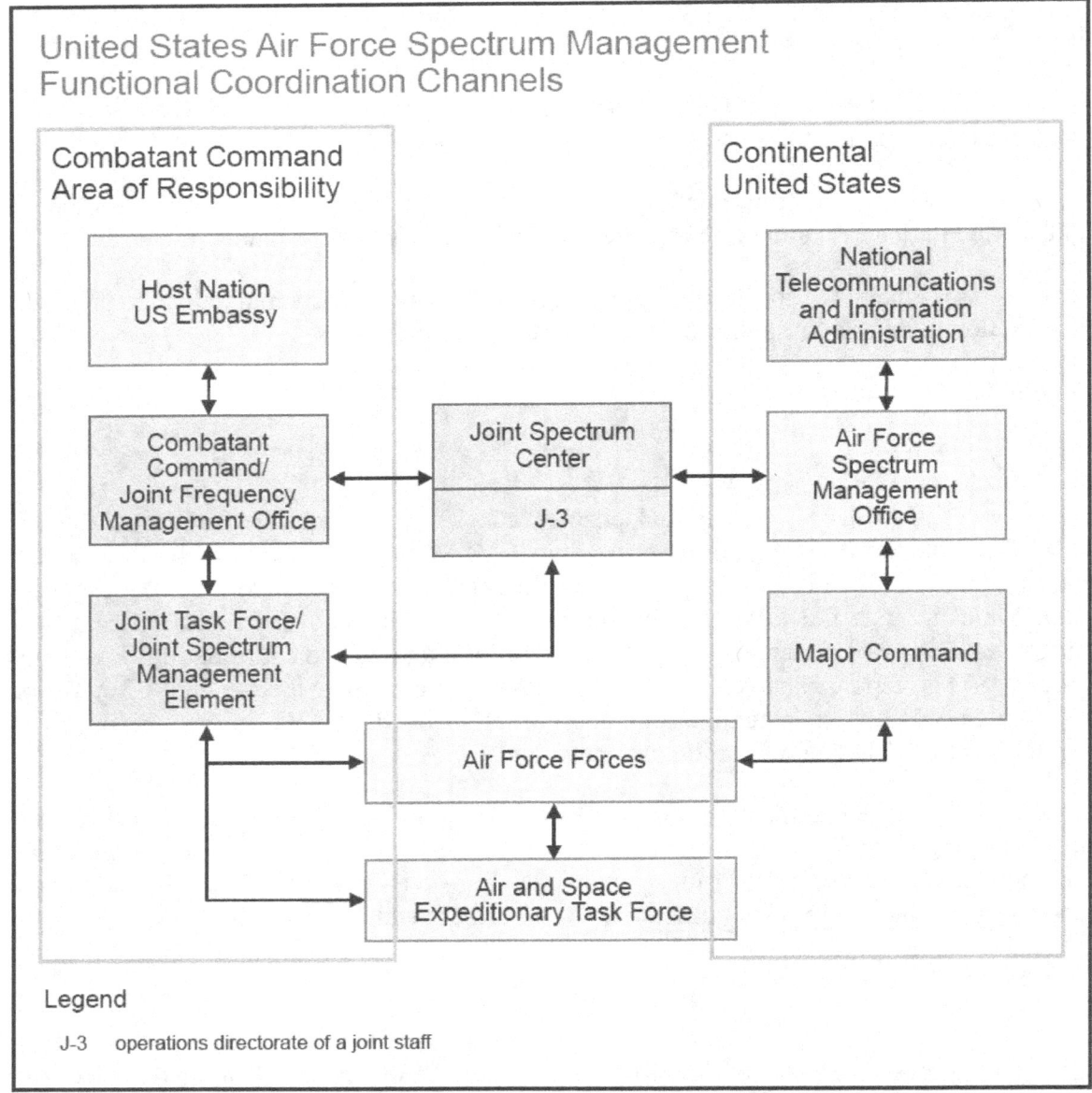

**Figure IV-2. United States Air Force Spectrum Management
Functional Coordination Channels**

For more information concerning Army spectrum organization, see Field Manual 6-02.70, Army Electromagnetic Spectrum Operations.

c. Marine Corps

The Commandant of the Marine Corps is responsible for spectrum supportability, including system/equipment spectrum certification and the allocation, assignment, and protection of all radio frequencies within the Marine Corps. Marine Corps force commanders provide operating forces and capabilities in support of the JFC. Marine Corps forces, installations, organizations, and activities coordinate SM support with the JFC via their respective Marine Corps Service component.

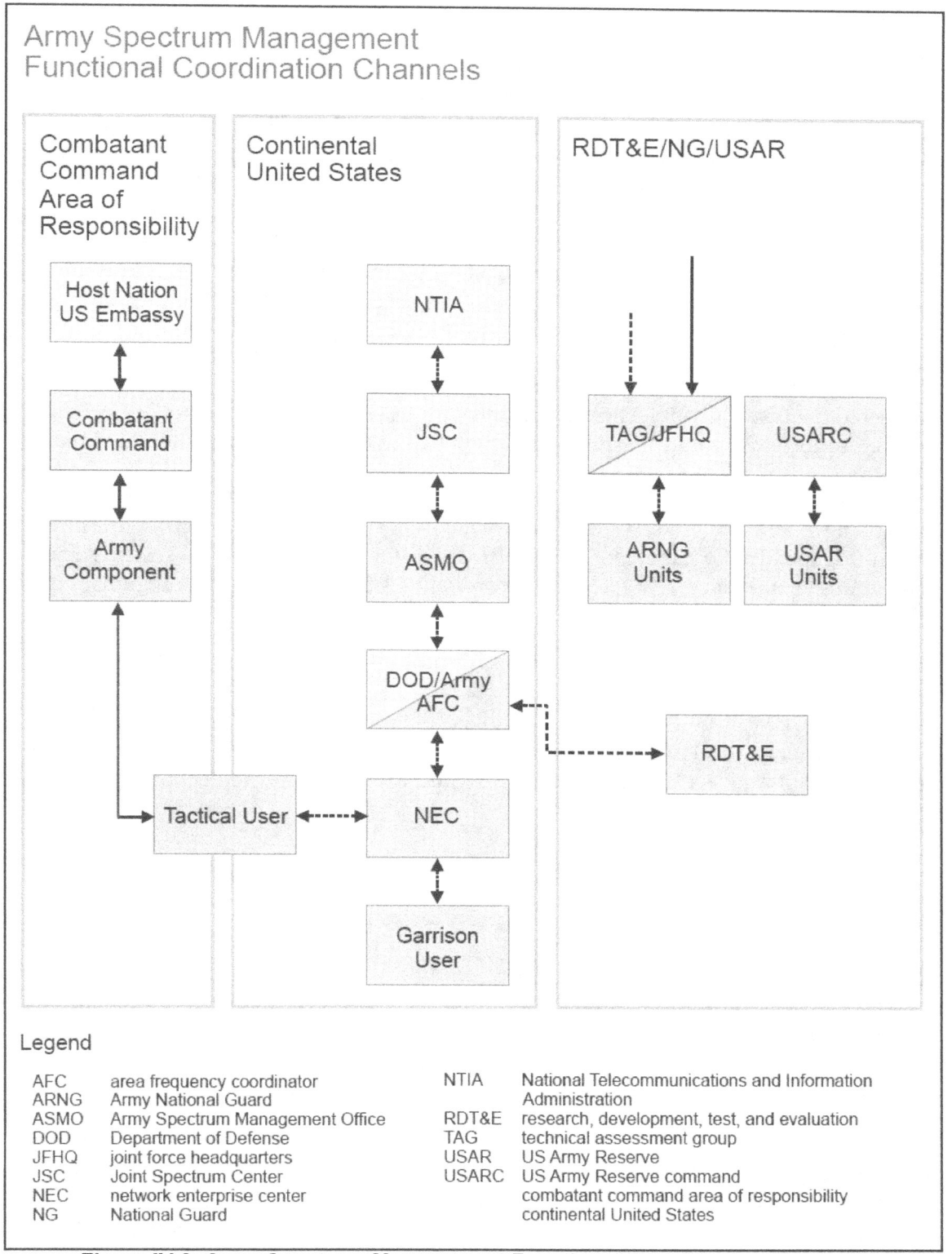

Figure IV-3. Army Spectrum Management Functional Coordination Channels

d. **Navy**

(1) The NMSC provides the Chief of Naval Operations spectrum supportability, including system/equipment spectrum certification and the allocation, assignment, and protection of all RF within the Navy. The Deputy Chief of Naval Operations for Information Dominance has delegated the responsibility for spectrum supportability and the management of the RF spectrum to Navy Cyber Forces (NAVCYBERFOR). NAVCYBERFOR has established the NMSC as the center of excellence for day-to-day spectrum certification and RF SM in support of all Navy and Marine Corps activities. Figure IV-4 depicts typical Navy and Marine Corps coordination channels. Consult Naval Telecommunications Procedures-6, *Navy Electromagnetic Spectrum (EMS) Guide,* for specific NMCS office geographic region of responsibilities.

(2) NMSC has established eight regional NMCSOs to support CCMDs and numbered fleets worldwide. The eight regional offices are located in Norfolk, Virginia; San Diego, California; Bangor, Washington; Honolulu, Hawaii; Guam, Japan, Italy, and Bahrain.

(3) For tactical operations, the Navy commander assigns responsibility for developing operation tasks (OPTASKs), which specify frequencies and constraints for spectrum-dependent equipment. The OPTASKs for communications systems and for combat systems (radars, EW, etc.), are coordinated with the appropriate regional NMCS office.

e. **Coast Guard**

(1) JEMSMO supports and enables all USCG responsibilities and duties as delineated under Title 10, USC, and Title 14, USC, by enabling spectrum interoperability with international, federal, DOD, state, local, and tribal agencies to accomplish its stated missions:

(a) Maritime safety (marine safety and search and rescue);

(b) Maritime security (drug and migrant interdiction, port waterways and coastal security);

(c) Maritime stewardship (marine resources, environmental protection, aids to navigation, ice operations); and

(d) National defense and DOD interoperability.

(2) The Spectrum Management Division supports JEMSMO by having trained personnel well-versed in joint operations. USCG, whether as the lead Service/agency or supporting international, DOD, or federal operations, understands agency unique spectrum planning, coordination, and operational parameters to be an effective member of the joint team. Figure IV-5 shows the USCG processes spectrum requirements for operations in the US and its territories and international operations.

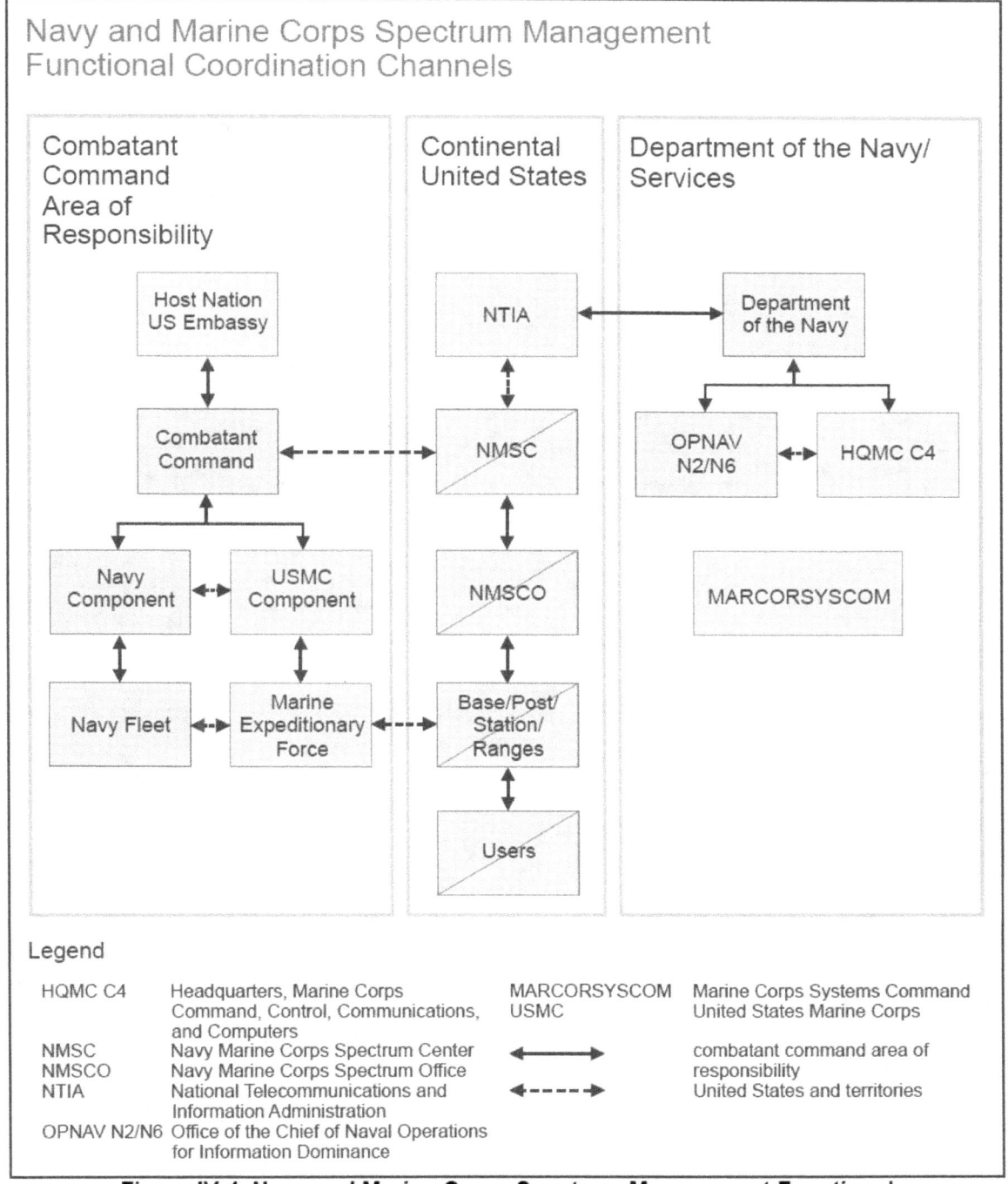

Figure IV-4. Navy and Marine Corps Spectrum Management Functional Coordination Channels

(3) The USCG is a military, multi-mission, maritime Service within the Department of Homeland Security and one of the nation's five armed Services. JEMSMO supports USCG's core roles to protect the public, the environment, and US economic and security interests in any maritime region in which those interests may be at risk, including international waters and America's coasts, ports, and inland waterways. The USCG provides

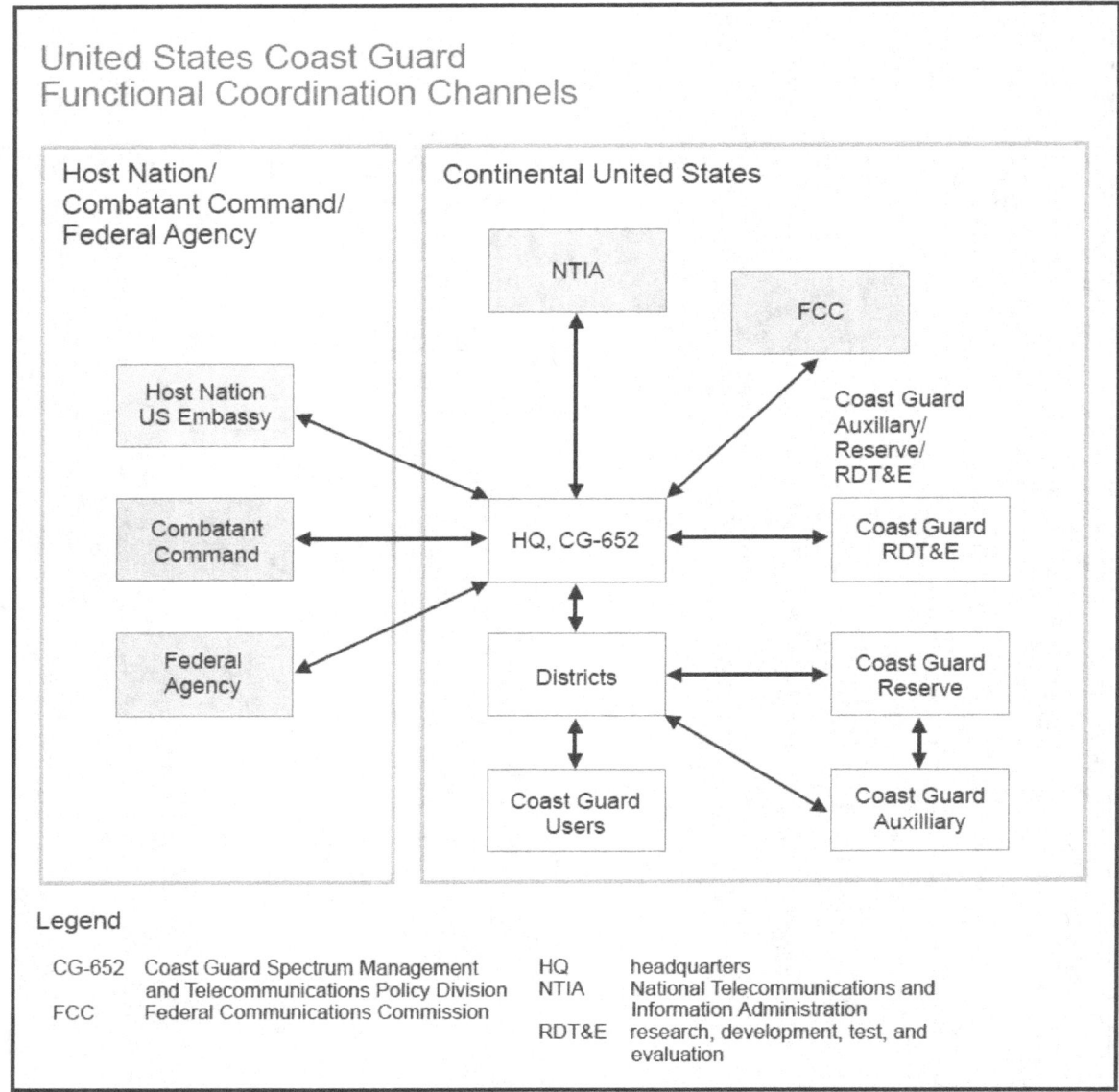

Figure IV-5. United States Coast Guard Functional Coordination Channels

unique benefits to the nation because of its distinctive blend of military, humanitarian, and civilian law enforcement capabilities.

f. **National Guard Bureau**

(1) The 54 NG JFHQ-States and territories are supported with frequency assignments by the ASMO through AFMO-CONUS. Frequency assignments for daily Air National Guard (ANG) aircraft and air support operations are supported by the AFSMO.

(2) NG forces in state active duty or Title 32, USC, status will submit frequency requests through these channels. NG forces in Title 10, USC, or federal status will submit requests for spectrum resources through elements of USNORTHCOM.

CHAPTER V
PLANNING JOINT ELECTROMAGNETIC SPECTRUM OPERATIONS

1. Introduction

a. SM is a complex mission area within modern military and civil operations that must be **fully integrated** with other aspects of joint operations in order to achieve its full potential for contributing to an operation's objectives. Such integration requires **careful planning.** SM planners must coordinate their **activities with other aspects of military operations** that use the EMS, as well as third-party users, to avoid disruption of services. Coordination of military EMS use is largely a matter of coordinating with other staff functions (primarily the J-2 and J-3) and components (to include multinational partners) that rely on the EMS to accomplish their mission. Coordination of SM activities, in the context of third-party EMS use, is largely a matter of SM and adherence to established frequency usage regimens and protocols. It is imperative that SM be elevated to the forefront in planning military operations to ensure effective use of the EMS.

> **Based on lessons learned in Iraq and Afghanistan, a lack of adherence to SM integration coupled with a lack of real-time SM, had an adverse effect on friendly communications.**

b. Like other aspects of joint operations, joint SM uses centralized planning and decentralized execution. Since the Services provide most of the assets available in joint operations, **Service component SM planners must be integrated into the joint planning process.** The JFC may delegate SM authorities to a component commander or lower echelon. However, such delegation does not eliminate the requirement for joint and/or multinational coordination of SM operations.

2. Planning Considerations

To use the spectrum successfully, all users must work together by exchanging vital spectrum information from the beginning of the joint planning process through an approved DOD data exchange architecture. Primarily, personnel assigned to the J-2, J-3, and J-6 staff sections plan, coordinate, and control joint military use of the EMS. To minimize unacceptable EMI among all emitters and receivers and to address E3 issues such as HERO in joint operations, these staff sections must work together. Additionally, automated SM systems at the joint and component levels require vertical and horizontal interoperability.

a. **Joint Spectrum Coordination.** Considerations are dependent upon the JTF mission, operational environment, and commander's intent. The size and depth of the JTF SM concept depends upon the planning process in which the EMSM is involved and how much time will be allowed for the completion of the planning task (i.e., planning would allow more time to define policy and guidance). Time for planning may be limited, and tasks will have to be prioritized. Items left unaddressed will negatively affect the quality of the JSME product. The types of information that should be considered in the SM concept are outlined below.

    (1) Multinational operations:

        (a) Types and numbers of spectrum-dependent equipment.

        (b) Information releasability.

        (c) Level of familiarity and experience in combined operations.

        (d) Availability of trained EMSMs.

        (e) Effective frequency assignment process.

        (f) Compatible data exchange format and processes.

        (g) JRFL sharing and releasability issues, multiple JRFLs, etc.

    (2) Spectrum-use considerations:

        (a) Type of operations.

        (b) Force complement.

        (c) Type of entry.

        (d) Area of responsibility.

        (e) Types of radio services.

        (f) Centralized or decentralized frequency assignment authority.

        (g) Spectrum coordination/availability.

        (h) Spectrum sharing for radios.

        (i) Threats to friendly spectrum.

        (j) Environmental factors.

        (k) Terrain.

        (l) Non-communications systems' spectrum use (e.g., friendly radars, missiles, EW, intelligence).

        (m) Cultural implications.

        (n) EW interference outside the AOR.

    (3) Resources:

        (a) Type/version of automated SM software.

(b) Compatible software and data formats.

(c) Secure connectivity to components.

(d) Capability to manage mobile, wide-area spectrum assignments.

(e) Is there sufficient bandwidth to support data exchange?

(f) Do bandwidth limitations affect decisions on types/formats of automated spectrum data to exchange?

(4) Interoperability. Interoperability is essential in order to use the SM process effectively as an element of joint military power. The major requirements of interoperability are to:

(a) Establish standards and practice procedures that allow for integrated planning and execution of SM.

(b) Exchange SM information in a timely and routine fashion. This exchange may be conducted in real time or near real time via common, secure, reliable means. The exchange of data relates to SM, JSIR, FM, and HNC, including friendly and adversary force data. Routine exchange of data among joint force components, the joint force, and supporting commands and organizations, and when possible allies and coalition partners, greatly facilitates all areas of SM planning.

b. **Restrictions.** Restrictions constitute SM issues that may not be under the control of SM planners. Some categories of restrictions include:

(1) Policy. HN agreements and command guidance may limit the flexibility of frequencies used. Laws, rules, policies, and guidelines become especially critical during peacetime operations when international and domestic laws, treaty provisions, and agreements, such as SOFAs, may affect SM planning and execution. Commanders should seek legal review at all levels of SM planning. This can best be accomplished by ensuring a legal advisor is available to SM planners.

(2) Meteorological and Oceanographic (METOC) restrictions. SM planners should consider the effects of atmospherics and space weather. For example, atmospheric inversions can propagate radio transmissions; high humidity and rainy climates are detrimental to satellite signals; and ionospheric scintillation can adversely affect Global Positioning System accuracy. Some atmospheric effects are well known and are categorized by season and location. Planners should consult with the CCMD METOC officer to determine the type of METOC support available for their operation.

3. Planning Process

The planning process for JEMSMO is conducted within the joint operation planning process (JOPP) and is designed to produce the products necessary for the commander to make timely decisions and aid in course of action (COA) development. Figure V-1 illustrates the JEMSMO planning process and the general correlation with the JOPP.

Joint Electromagnetic Spectrum Management Operations Planning Process

Input	Joint Electromagnetic Spectrum Management Operations Planning Activity	Output/Product	Joint Operation Planning Process Step
Known, existing spectrum requirements Commander's guidance Existing policy Doctrine Civilian frequencies Any known enemy frequencies	Define policy and guidance	Spectrum operations concept Data call message	Initiation
Data call message User spectrum requirements	Gather spectrum requirements	Spectrum database	Initiation
Database of requirements	Develop the spectrum requirements summary	JTF spectrum requirements	Initiation
All JTF frequencies, including combat systems, air/sea navigation aids, and radars EW and intelligence considerations Terrain Environmental considerations	Joint preparation of the electromagnetic operational environment	Spectrum operations limitations Staff estimate	Mission analysis
JTF spectrum requirements	Obtain spectrum resources and host nation coordination	JTF spectrum allotment	COA processes
All previous information	Develop the spectrum operations plan	Spectrum appendix to plan	Plan or order development

LEGEND
COA   course of action
EW   electronic warfare
JTF   joint task force

Figure V-1. Joint Electromagnetic Spectrum Management Operations Planning Process

a. **Define Policy and Guidance**

(1) In order to be fully integrated into a planned operation, the EMSM conducts planning as early as possible and coordinates it with other aspects of the plan throughout the planning process. The type of plan, expected length, geographic location, time allotted for planning, and level of hostilities expected during the operation will help to determine the scope of the SM planner's effort.

(2) The JFMO should be the resource center for the JSME throughout its lifetime since the JFMO has extensive institutional knowledge concerning the GCC's AOR spectrum issues. The JFMO should prepare the basic SM resources needed to establish a JSME in support of operations anywhere within the GCC's AOR. Such resources should include digitized terrain data, background EME records, country area studies, copies of agreements for spectrum use or sharing with involved or adjacent HNs, and historical spectrum-use records involving the JTF operational area. There are two deliverable products generated with this activity: the JTF SM concept and the **spectrum requirements data call message.**

(3) The **SM concept** is the vision of how SM operations would best be performed to support the JTF mission. The SM concept comprises assumptions, considerations, and restrictions that, when analyzed together, can illustrate the best approach to managing the JTF EMOE for joint/multinational forces. The command/JTF J-2 can provide further mission-related information on the current situation. The EWC, if activated, or the command EWO can provide information concerning EW operations being contemplated.

(4) Planning requires the use of assumptions to accomplish the mission. It is important to document all assumptions made during the planning process so that, if the resulting plan is implemented, the JFMO/JSME using the plan will know what assumptions were used to make decisions in the development of the OPLAN or CONPLAN. Assumptions may have to be made concerning resources and the availability of personnel, equipment, connectivity, and information. To continue planning and making decisions, the EMSM may be forced to make educated assumptions based on the most likely scenario. Based on the nature of the mission, the EMSM will also make assumptions on the participation of multinational forces, possibility of HN coordination, type of entry (forcible or unopposed), and the availability of spectrum resources. Assumptions should not replace information that can be obtained. Assumptions made to expedite the decision-making process do so at the expense of accuracy. Because planning is a continual process, these assumptions should be replaced by facts when they become available.

(5) The JTF spectrum requirements data call message provides guidance to JTF staff elements, components, and supporting agencies on how to request spectrum support for spectrum-dependent systems that operate under their control within the JTF's AOI. The data call message typically includes the following:

(a) JTF SM policy and guidance.

(b) Security classification guidance.

<u>1</u>. Procedures for requesting frequencies to support spectrum-dependent equipment, including lead times and request format.

<u>2</u>. SM automation system and configuration.

<u>3.</u> JCEOI master net list (MNL) requirements collection process, including the need for identifying nets requiring call signs, call words, and possible frequency sharing.

<u>4</u>. JRFL submission procedures, including lead times and restrictions.

b. **Gather Spectrum Requirements**

(1) Gathering requirements can begin as soon as SM guidance is received and coordination channels are defined. The JFMO/JSME should first obtain any records available, such as ITU records, JSC country studies, HN records, and any civil allocation tables or frequency channel plans. While in the past, the concentration was on communications systems, these requirements must address both communications and non-communications (radar, weapons, etc.) systems.

(2) The JSME should be proactive in engaging the staff, units, and organizations in identifying spectrum requirements. This initial contact introduces spectrum users to the JSME. The primary JTF staff elements involved in JEMSMO planning are the J-2, J-3, and J-6; however, in today's wireless rich environment, all staff elements and units should be queried regarding their spectrum requirements and be considered in the planning process. This proactive approach will pay dividends in reduced interference problems later.

(3) Service components should identify all requirements for spectrum-dependent systems that they bring to the JTF. However, there are always items missed and systems overlooked in coordinating spectrum use. The best approach to gathering requirements is to attend operations briefings, meetings, and planning sessions. These venues will provide information about new units arriving, new systems being deployed, and changes to the operational plan. All of these activities are indications of new or changed spectrum usage and need to be included in the frequency assignment database.

(4) EMS-dependent systems that are designed as receive-only should be included in the data call. The way to identify these systems is to talk to the JTF staff sections to request that they identify any receive-only systems that they know are active or plan on activating. Such systems include passive sensors and RF identification devices. The EMSM can then create frequency records for these receivers and afford them protection when nominating frequencies and performing interference analysis.

(5) In order to mitigate interference to satellite systems, the spectrum requirements data call message should include instruction to the components regarding notification to the JSME on all satellite access requests and authorizations. Users must obtain a local frequency clearance in addition to the authorization for satellite use. The JSME can then create frequency records for these authorizations which will afford protection for the satellite systems.

(6) Gathering requirements also involves capturing and documenting potential JTF spectrum use identified by the Service components and JTF staff, as well as undocumented requirements from sources external to the SM coordination chain. Using the previously developed spectrum requirements data call message, the JSME requests that spectrum requirements and JCEOI MNL for all units and organizations supporting the JTF be submitted. The data call message requires units to submit their spectrum requests to the CCMD JFMO or JSME. Gathering requirements is an on-going activity that continues until the JTF is dissolved.

(7) The product generated by this activity is a database containing the known JTF spectrum requirements.

c. **Develop the Spectrum Requirements Summary**

(1) Once the database is populated with the requirements, the JSME will develop the spectrum requirements summary. This summary is used to quantify the amount of spectrum necessary to support the JTF, determine the necessity of using frequency sharing and reuse plans, and help in the development of allotment or channeling plans. For radars, the available band assignment must be distributed among the numerous and various systems. These processes require manipulating the data previously gathered and translating it into a format that will facilitate analysis. The EMSM analyzes the spectrum requirements summary and draws conclusions concerning the amount of spectrum required to support the JTF. In addition, the JSME determines the number of radio services competing for spectrum in the same frequency band, determines the different emissions utilizing a particular band, and develops a plan for frequency sharing.

(2) The spectrum requirements summary generated with this activity is a compilation of the requirements identified in response to the spectrum requirements data call message. This product is for the sole use of the EMSM and provides a tool in which to base future decisions about efficient spectrum use and initial requirements definition. This product may assist the EMSM in requesting spectrum from an HN or provide insight into how to better allocate portions of the spectrum to support emitters utilizing varying bandwidths.

(3) The EMSM must also consider the anticipated growth or length of the operation being planned. Additional frequencies or channels may be needed for expansion or changes in missions.

d. **Define the Electromagnetic Operational Environment**

(1) Joint operations in a net-centric environment inherently employ a large number of spectrum-dependent devices that span all phases and types of military operations. Joint operations require a common, single, authoritative source for spectrum-use information for all friendly, enemy (to the extent available), neutral, and civil emitters and receivers to achieve and manage successful joint spectrum use. This common source of spectrum-use information must be current, accurate, and accessible to authorized users. The JSME is responsible for building and managing this common source of information. Because of the

amount and complexity of spectrum-use information typically involved in joint operations, modern computer and communications networking systems are needed to maintain, analyze, and distribute this common spectrum-use information. When working with allied, United Nations, or multinational forces, the JSME should obtain similar information from each to maximize effective use and control of the spectrum throughout the AOR.

(2) Defining the EMOE is not only creating a database of frequency assignments, but also identifying factors that affect signal propagation, such as environmental characteristics and terrain. This activity starts with defining the AOI and its environmental characteristics, locating necessary terrain data, and creating a database of the known spectrum-use information. This process also includes updating and maintaining this spectrum-use information as well as adding all JTF frequency assignments. The JSME should use the common spectrum-use database generated in gathering requirements for planning and coordinating control of the EMOE. Once the EMOE is defined, it can be used as the staff estimate for mission analysis in the joint planning process. During crisis action or deliberate planning, certain assumptions may have to be made to provide an initial estimate, which will be revised as operational planning unfolds. Defining the EMOE is an ongoing activity until the JTF is dissolved.

e. **Obtain Spectrum Resources**

(1) Once the EMS requirement is identified, the JSME must obtain EMS resources needed to support the JTF. IAW J-5 guidance, the JSME will also coordinate military spectrum use with the spectrum authority of the HN(s) or multinational forces involved. Spectrum resources can be requested from the HNs for exercises or stability operations such as peace building or humanitarian missions. Operations that preclude prior coordination with an HN, such as offensive operations, require the JSME to determine the spectrum resource. If an evaluation of the background environment is required, it is essential to establish well-defined spectrum requirements and for the EMOE to be as completely defined and up-to-date as possible. This process is an ongoing activity and is expected to continue until the JTF is dissolved.

(2) Products generated in previous activities can help in determining the amount of spectrum needed to support the JTF mission. The spectrum requirements summary can help quantify the amount of spectrum needed and identify the radio services and emissions that will be operating within each frequency band. Spectrum resources are normally created and stored as one or more allotment plans.

(3) **Host Nation Coordination Considerations**

(a) The JFMO has standing coordination channels in place with the nations in the GCC's AOR. These may fluctuate from time to time, and in some cases, there may be an absence of formal coordination channels. When this occurs, the JFMO may delegate HN coordination to the JSME. The JFMO/JSME must ensure subordinate elements do not engage in HN coordination without the approval of the JFMO/JSME. HN coordination is normally based on the fostering of mutual trust and rapport between the JFMO and the HN.

Outside attempts at coordination may disrupt or damage this relationship, making support more difficult to obtain.

(b) Effective HN coordination requires not only a technical understanding of how a nation manages its spectrum resource but also a cultural understanding in order to procure the necessary spectrum required for the commander to conduct operations. The following provide some considerations to facilitate successful HN coordination.

1. Review HN allocation/channel plan and usage/broadcast schedules.

2. Compare joint force emitters with the HN channel plan to see where potential problems exist.

a. Does the equipment meet the allocation table (i.e., emission bandwidth and type of service)?

b. Is there enough spectrum in the band to support the JFC requirement?

3. Devise coordination plan.

a. Arrange to meet with HN representative.

b. Be aware of customs and culture.

c. Use tact and courtesy to gain full cooperation.

d. Show genuine concern for HN concerns but remain resolute in obtaining the maximum resource and flexibility for JFC operations.

e. Prepare request according to HN guidelines.

f. Maintain accurate records of all dialogue and agreements made with HN.

4. Prepare command brief of HN agreement status and the mitigation strategy or COAs for concerns or shortfalls.

f. **Develop the Spectrum Management Plan**

(1) The JSME is responsible for establishing JTF-specific guidance for managing, requesting, coordinating, and assigning EMS use, JRFL process, JCEOI, and other processes. Additionally, they are the focal point for inclusion of spectrum-use considerations in annex K development and for providing administrative and technical support for military spectrum use. This process uses the SM concept, developed in the first activity, along with existing CCMD JFMO policy and guidance. Other sources of information are previous operations and exercises, the JSC, other EMSMs, and all of an EMSM's SM training and experience. The JTF EMSM will devise a plan to effectively and efficiently use the spectrum resources

available. The primary guidance will devolve from the commander's operational approach utilizing the JOPP. The JTF EMSM will also be guided by experiences, advice from the JFMO, and other SM sources. This plan depends upon the products of all the previous activities. The SM plan is evaluated and revised continuously as operations evolve.

(2) The SM plan provides guidance for all JTF SM functions and specifies how those interactions will be conducted, information exchanged, expected coordination, and format for deliverable products to users. This plan will also document how to address interference problems, reporting procedures, and suggested resolution steps. This plan will normally become the spectrum operations appendices of annex K to the OPLANs or similar documents.

4. Coordination with Network Operations, Electronic Warfare, and Intelligence

a. The JRFL is developed prior to initiating JTF operations and is continually modified during operations. The JRFL is a time, frequency, and geographically oriented listing of functions, nets, and frequencies requiring protection from friendly EW. Adversary communications nets being exploited are referred to as GUARDED, and safety-of-life frequencies being used by the JTF and local civil noncombatants are referred to as TABOO. Each of the frequencies, nets, etc., should have a priority listing within the main categories of PROTECTED, GUARDED, or TABOO.

b. Coordination with Network Operations

(1) Network operations (NETOPS) are DOD activities conducted to operate and defend the DOD information networks. The purpose of NETOPS is to provide the JFC with assured system and network availability, assured information protection, and assured information delivery. The effectiveness of NETOPS is measured in terms of availability and reliability. The J-6 is responsible for both NETOPS and JEMSMO. While there is overlap of the two functions, it is important to distinguish that they are two separate functions and that they are planned, managed, and executed independently. The portion of overlap between NETOPS and JEMSMO is between the FM portion of JEMSMO and the NETOPS essential task, DOD information networks management.

(2) NETOPS is addressed much the same as any other user of the EMS. NETOPS tools used to assign frequencies for the network should also determine the spectrum requirement (frequencies) for the network and provide this information to the spectrum manager in the approved DOD format. Once the spectrum manager receives the requirement, the SM portion of JEMSMO will be performed to determine if adequate resources are currently available or will have to be requested through CCMD or HN channels. Once the frequency resource is identified, it must meet policy compliance in the AOR and be deconflicted among all other users. The spectrum manager will then provide this approved allotment of frequencies to NETOPS in the same DOD-approved format. Once the frequencies have been assigned, the NETOPS tool provides a spectrum (frequency) use report back to the JEMSMO tool so that continual analysis can be done as the network moves or frequencies within the network are reassigned.

c. Coordination with Electronic Warfare

(1) At CCMDs and subordinate unified commands, coordination for EW will normally be handled through the JFC's EW staff or the joint EWC. The EWC may be assigned to the J-3 and normally consists of members from the primary staff sections, a fires officer, and an EMSM. The EMSM participates and represents JEMSMO issues.

(2) The JFMO/JSME should ensure participation in any EW planning in order to reduce, mitigate, or eliminate undesired EW effects on other JEMSO. The proliferation of friendly EA systems has made this participation critical for the execution of JEMSMO.

(3) If the EWC cannot adequately reduce, mitigate, or eliminate undesired EW effects on other JEMSO, the JFMO/JSME will provide an analysis stating the impact on JEMSO and a recommendation to the JFC. The JFC, or his designated representative, will decide which COA for EM maneuver to pursue. See Figure V-2.

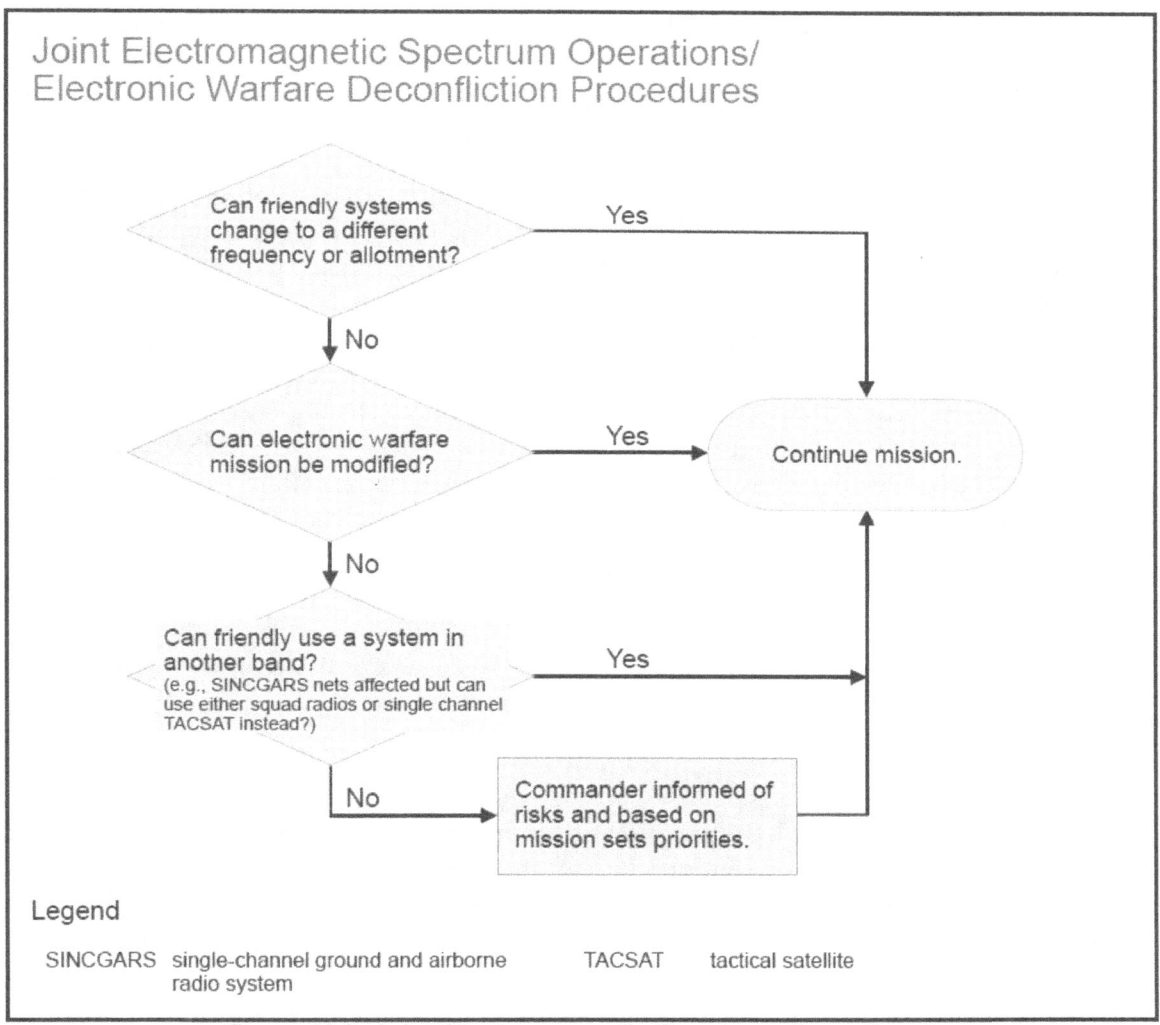

**Figure V-2. Joint Electromagnetic Spectrum Operations/
Electronic Warfare Deconfliction Procedures**

(4) To aid in EMS deconfliction, planners should participate in a joint targeting coordination board or like body, as appropriate, to apply offensive EW capabilities against targets on the commander's joint integrated prioritized target list.

d. Coordination with Intelligence

(1) Coordination with intelligence units and agencies can be challenging for many reasons, to include classification issues, disparate data formats, and separate technical control or reporting channels. In many cases, the JSME does not have adequate visibility or knowledge of intelligence sensors, platforms, or systems in order to accomplish accurate deconfliction. Integrating intelligence staff and entities in all JEMSMO and JSME planning activities is crucial to effective operations preparation.

(2) The JRFL is the primary mechanism that enables coordination with intelligence. The JRFL largely deals with signals intelligence (SIGINT); however, in order to capture all aspects of intelligence spectrum use, the JSME must understand that intelligence platforms such as UAS/unmanned ground system will have spectrum requirements for both a payload (e.g., imagery or data) and control frequencies to operate the platform. Intelligence is a heavy user of sensors that employ both active and passive techniques. Active sensors are usually accounted for, but the passive sensors will also require spectrum consideration so they perform properly.

(3) The IC can be a valuable source of spectrum information. The SIGINT discipline of intelligence utilizes a vast network of sensors and electronic signals collection systems. Also, the IC may have information about an adversary's efforts in collecting spectrum data from allied systems. This information can be useful in developing spectrum plans that minimize the spectrum data available to an adversary. While the IC works to exploit both foreign communications systems and non-communications emitters, JEMSMO is concerned with efficient use and control of the spectrum. The two major obstructions to JEMSMO utilizing this information are classification and data format. EMSMs at the joint level should have the security clearance required and the appropriate access to vital IC spectrum information. Another limitation of intelligence spectrum data is that it is threat focused, whereas JEMSMO considers the entire EMOE. The EWC and IO cell are key nodes in the effort to overcome these issues. Joint spectrum operators must work toward standardizing and sharing this data among the intelligence, EW, combat systems, communications, and spectrum communities. This holistic view of the spectrum is required to inform the commanders' common operational picture.

5. Major Operations and Campaigns Planning

a. Major operations and campaigns are the most complex and require the greatest diligence in planning and execution due to the time, effort, and national resources committed. Major operations and campaigns, whether or not they involve large-scale combat, normally will include some level of both offense and defense (e.g., interdiction, maneuver, forcible entry, fire support, counter-air, computer network defense, and base defense).

b. Offensive operations, particularly those that require movement over significant distances, represent the greatest challenges to spectrum operators. This is largely attributable to the manual intervention required to maintain spectrum databases. Since it may not be possible to accurately track maneuver force spectrum, the JSME will likely address spectrum issues as they arise rather than be proactive in the planning. In order to mitigate these occurrences, the JSME should have representation in all key planning forums.

c. Due to the magnitude of major operations, the planning activities that will pose the biggest challenges are gathering requirements and defining the EMOE. Major operations require that the JSME have representation from each of the Services in order to fully develop the spectrum database. Most restraints or constraints in major operations and campaign planning will be internal. The JFC will fight the adversary to gain and maintain the freedom to maneuver. The JSME will be required to manage the density and variety of users requiring spectrum during these types of operations.

d. Full spectrum operations may require that planning be conducted simultaneously for offensive, defensive, and stability operations. Most important, planning for stability operations should begin when joint operation planning is initiated. Planning for the transition from sustained combat operations to the termination of joint operations and then a complete handover to civil authority and redeployment must commence during plan development and be ongoing during all phases of a campaign or major operation.

e. Stability operations seek to maintain or reestablish a safe and secure environment and provide essential governmental services, emergency infrastructure reconstruction, or humanitarian relief. Proper SM and discipline are crucial to both political and economic stabilization, and the JFMO/JSME may take part in helping to reestablish national spectrum authority for a nation. The JFMO/JSME should understand the allocation tables for the region, to include channeling plans for critical services such as public safety, phone, public radio, and TV. Stability operations support USG plans for stability, security, transition, and reconstruction operations and likely will be conducted in coordination with and in support of HN authorities, other government departments and agencies, intergovernmental organizations (IGOs) and/or NGOs, and the private sector.

6. Crisis Response and Limited Contingency Operations Planning

a. Due to the nature of these types of operations, the approach to spectrum planning will vary greatly and will typically be very compressed. If joint forces are already in place, such as a noncombatant evacuation operation from South Korea, then planning may have already been done or be minimal. In nearly all cases, coordination will be critical with HNs, adjacent nations if staging areas are required, or local, state, and federal agencies in the case of HD and CS operations.

b. Unlike major operations and campaign planning, crisis response and limited contingency operations planning will likely have significant external limitations and restrictions on the use of spectrum. Difficulty in coordination, HN restrictions, and non-compatible equipment will all constrain or restrict JEMSMO in these types of operations.

7. Military Engagement, Security Cooperation, and Deterrence Planning

Like crisis response and limited contingency operations planning, military engagement, security cooperation, and deterrence planning will likely have significant external limitations and restrictions on the use of spectrum. Because the Department of State is frequently the federal agency with lead responsibility and nearly always is a principal player in these activities, JFCs should maintain a working relationship with the chiefs of the US diplomatic missions in their area. The JFMO/JSME should establish contact and maintain a dialogue with pertinent other government departments and agencies, IGOs, and NGOs to share information and facilitate operations.

8. Homeland Defense/Defense Support of Civil Authorities Planning

a. DSCA/HD missions are likely to affect operations being conducted by other EMS users. The DSCA/HD mission requires an unprecedented level of interoperability and cooperation between federal, state, and local governments; civilian first responders; and the public.

b. JFMO NORTH is the designated office within the USNORTHCOM AOR responsible for planning and execution of SM for DSCA/HD assigned forces. It provides support to NG forces in Title 10, USC, status and forces planning or executing operations in support of the DSCA/HD mission. When contingency operations, missions, and training for joint and multinational exercises are in areas where GCCs' AORs intersect or are not clearly defined, JFMO NORTH will coordinate spectrum requirements with the respective CCMD JFMO.

c. During normal operations, NG forces in state active duty or Title 32, USC, status will submit their peacetime requirements through existing spectrum support channels (e.g., Army National Guard [ARNG] will submit through NG JFHQ-State to AFMO-CONUS, and ANG units will submit through the A-6 Spectrum Management Office to AFSMO). All JFMO NORTH component, supporting, and subordinate commands will submit frequency requests through JFMO NORTH. USNORTHCOM Title 10, USC, forces may be ordered into the impacted area by the President, normally at the request of the governor. USNORTHCOM spectrum manager will join the spectrum flyaway team (SFAT) to assist in coordinating/deconflicting spectrum issues at the lowest level possible. On request, spectrum managers will support the JTF formed of Title 10, USC, forces which are supporting the contingency. Frequency requests will go through the Title 10, USC, process. NG JFHQ-State continues to request frequencies through the NGB J-6 C4-SMB. Coordination with Title 10, USC, assets occurs through the SFAT. Both USNORTHCOM and NGB J-6 C4-SMB will request spectrum through the appropriate Service spectrum office. See Figure V-3 for a diagram of this relationship.

d. For contingencies and exercises, the North American Aerospace Defense Command/USNORTHCOM commander may direct the establishment of a JSME to support a Title 10, USC, JTF commander during exercises and contingencies IAW CJCSM 3320.01B, *Joint Operations in the Electromagnetic Battlespace*.

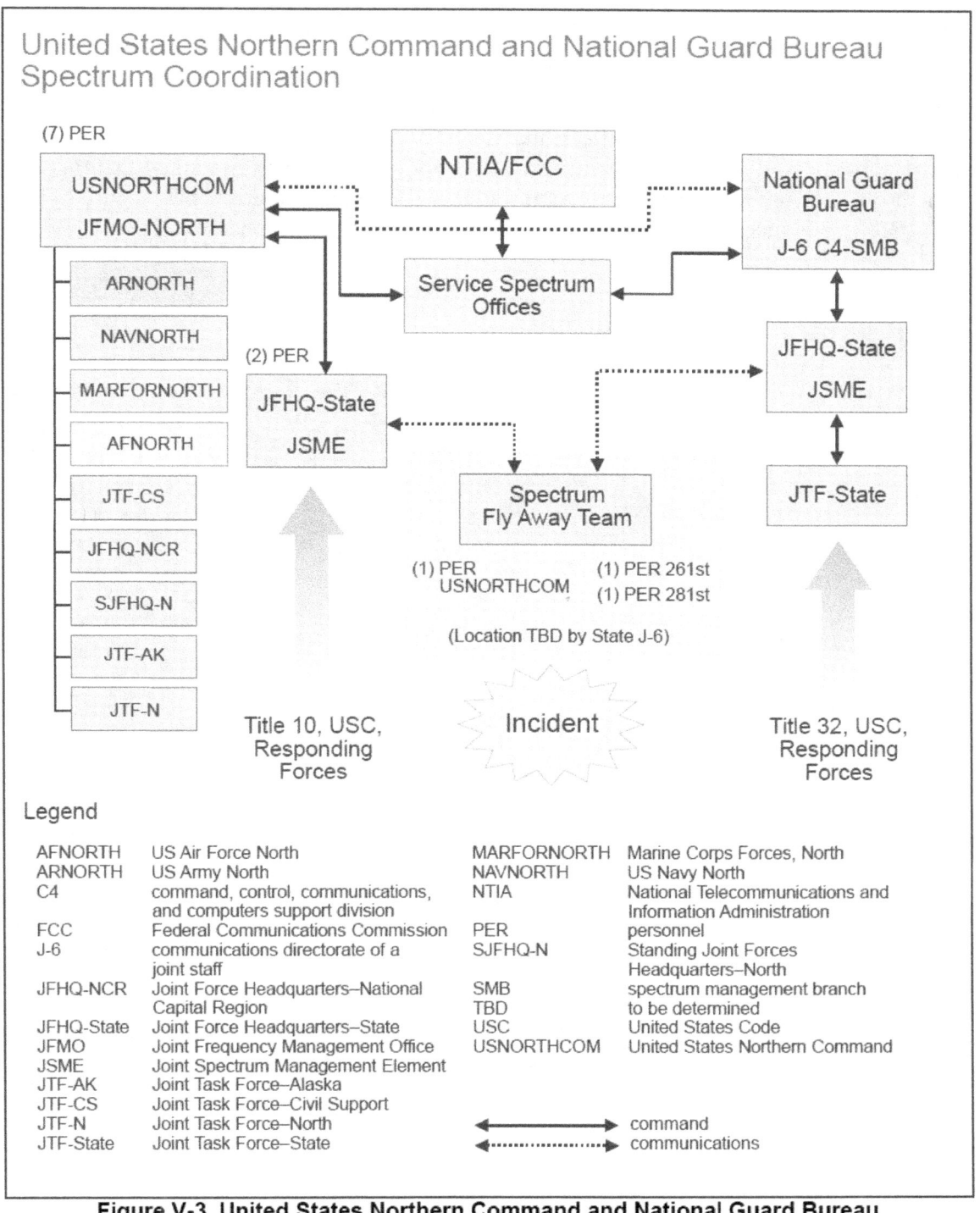

Figure V-3. United States Northern Command and National Guard Bureau Spectrum Coordination

e. Contingency OPLANs have been designed to provide a preplanned rapid response to virtually any event having an impact upon HD or DSCA. These OPLANs vary in type of response to cover events ranging from natural man-made and peaceful to hostile, and may require support from any or all HD or DSCA responders in support of other national federal or state agencies. The majority of contingency OPLANs identify the command structures and relationships involved in executing various options or phases contained therein. It is imperative that the basic spectrum requirements for implementation of an OPLAN are identified in advance and incorporated in that particular plan or appended thereto.

CHAPTER VI
CONDUCTING JOINT ELECTROMAGNETIC SPECTRUM OPERATIONS

1. Execute Electromagnetic Portion of Operational Plan

a. **Concept of Control.** The supported JFC holds the authority for assigning frequencies to users, usually through the JFMO/JSME. The JFMO/JSME may on occasion delegate frequency assignment authority to subordinate commands. Authority to assign use of a specific spectrum resource (use of allotment plans developed by the JFMO/JSME) should be delegated to the lowest level of command possible, consistent with the principles of sound SM, spectrum-use considerations, CONOPS, and priority of mission functions detailed in the respective Service or joint publications. Subordinate commands given authority for approving spectrum use will make frequency assignments within the constraints imposed by higher authorities and report changes in spectrum assignment information to the JFMO/JSME.

b. **Interference Resolution**

(1) To ensure critical frequencies and spectrum-dependent systems are protected from unintentional interference due to friendly operations, the JFMO/JSME will perform an interference analysis of all spectrum requests against existing frequency assignments to identify and deconflict potential interference before making a new assignment. As new requirements are identified, situations of conflicting or competing spectrum use will occur. Conflicts within a primary functional area should be resolved at the lowest possible level.

(2) Resolving interference is a daily activity once forces have deployed and is not a part of the planning process. The JSME is responsible for the analysis and attempts to resolve incidents of unacceptable EMI. This activity encompasses the resolution of, and reporting of, RF interference. Interference is a common problem that has many sources, and attempts should be made locally to resolve the interference. Interference incidents indicate the possibility of unauthorized users, faulty nomination criteria, lack of timely data exchanges, or equipment problems.

(3) Multiple interference problems may indicate adversary EW operations, unintentional impact of friendly EW operations, or errors in the JTF SM plan. The interference resolution process uses the EMOE to determine if the problem is something that was overlooked or was a miscalculation by the automated SM system.

(4) JSME should ensure users are aware of the reporting process through the JSIR program. Timely reporting of EMI would allow the JSME to determine if the EMI event was localized, regional, or transregional, and deploy assets to gather information as to possible causes. JSIR reports can also provide a basis of lessons learned to resolve other EMI events and identify potential changes in the JCEOI.

(5) The mechanism for addressing EMI is the JSIR program, which addresses EMI events and EW affecting DOD. The program is coordinated and centrally managed for the Joint Staff by the JSC, Annapolis, Maryland; however, the execution process is highly

decentralized. Each of the DOD components shares responsibility for successful execution of the JSIR program.

(a) The objective of the JSIR program is to report and assist with the resolution of recurring EMI. The four-step resolution process for EMI events:

1. Identification and verification.

2. Characterization and reporting.

3. Geolocation/direction finding.

4. Resolution.

(b) Resolution includes, but is not limited to, implementation of EMI corrective actions needed to regain use of the affected spectrum. However, some EMI events cease before corrective action is taken and, in other cases, the EMI corrections may not be feasible, affordable, or result in regaining the use of the spectrum.

(c) The JSIR program attempts to resolve EMI at the lowest possible level using organic and/or other assets available to the command. If an EMI event cannot be resolved locally, it must be elevated up the chain of command with each higher level attempting resolution. The JSC has direct liaison authority to coordinate, consult, and request information from other involved organizations as deemed necessary to resolve EMI. If the event cannot be resolved at the lowest level, CCDRs should determine the appropriate level to request direct support from the JSC. JSIR reports will aid in identifying possible causes for subsequent interference. To the extent unexplained interference persists or recurs coincident with suspected enemy operations, the EWC should be advised.

(6) The use of spectrum collection devices, such as a spectrum analyzer and analytical software, may further define and refine spectrum use. Through near-real-time analysis of the EMS, the EMSM can proactively mitigate harmful interference and utilize the EMS more efficiently. The information produced by this activity is a baseline database digitally depicting the EMOE and will be the basis for all JTF spectrum interaction analyses.

(7) New and experimental spectrum-dependent systems will be introduced as the JTF mission progresses; these new systems will need to be identified, evaluated, and coordinated as they arrive in the AOR. Situational awareness of new systems, additional forces, incidents of interference, and the movement or relocation of existing forces should be maintained by attending operational meetings, briefings, and planning sessions. JSME participation in all EWC and daily operations briefings benefits the JTF immensely. J-6 staff representation at the same meetings has been thought to negate the needs for the JSME EMSM to attend. The JSME representative, due to the involvement in operations not performed or conducted by the J-6, can often recognize issues and concerns dealing with SM that are not evident to others in the JCCC or the J-6.

c. **JEMSMO Considerations by Phase.** JEMSMO supports and enables full spectrum operations through all phases. The three functions of JEMSMO—FM, HNC, and JSIR—

could all be employed in any type of operation, but the phase of an operation will determine the focus of JEMSMO. Figure VI-1 illustrates a notional focus of JEMSMO through the phases of an operation.

(1) Shaping

(a) The shaping phase of an operation is concerned with building and strengthening relationships between future multinational partners, gaining a better understanding of the region, pursuing actions to ensure access when needed, and preventing crises. The emphasis of JEMSMO during the shaping phase is focused on HNC, adaptive planning, and studying potential adversaries.

(b) HNC is employed to gain a better understanding of the EMOE, which includes HN spectrum plans; rules for spectrum use; and geographical, physical, and environmental considerations, such as the effects of weather and terrain. Proactive HNC will provide joint forces with the necessary spectrum access to stage or train in the shaping phase, which enhances operational reach.

(c) Using lessons learned, the commander's objectives, HNC, and the threat environment, JEMSMO include developing the appropriate annexes for the theater OPLAN

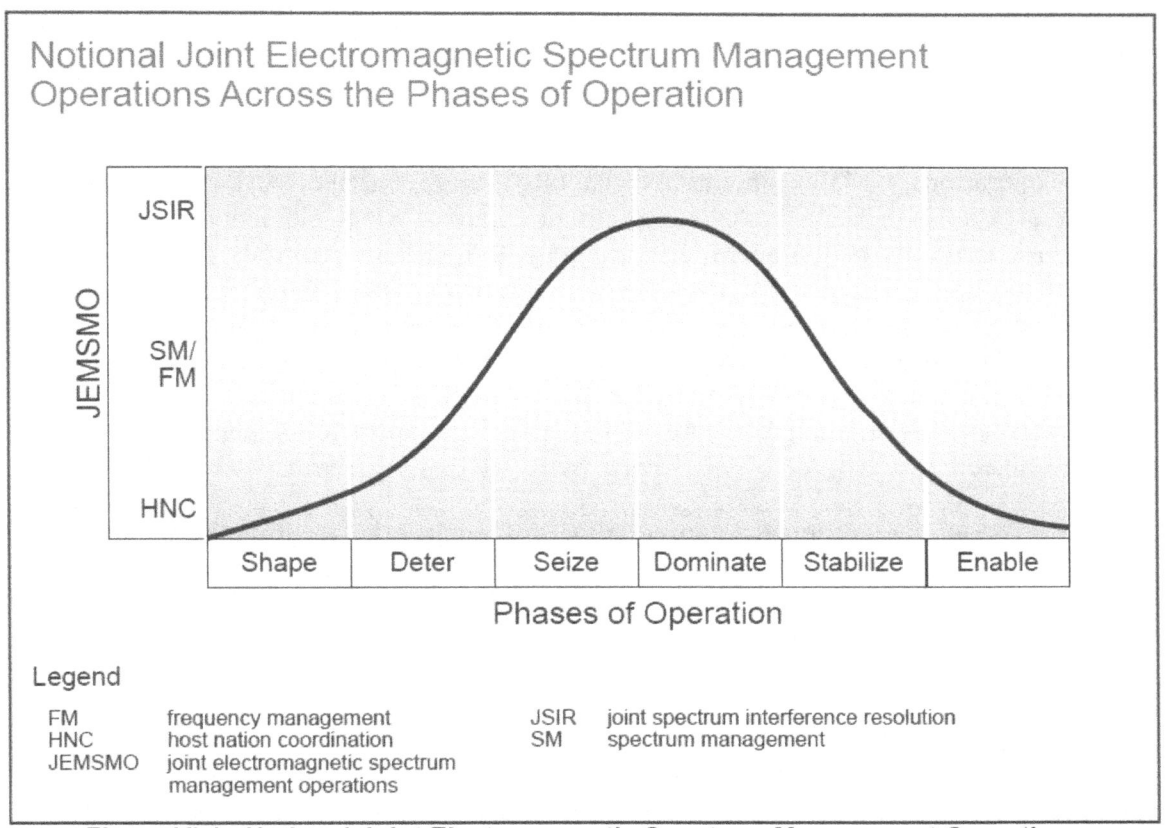

Figure VI-1. Notional Joint Electromagnetic Spectrum Management Operations Across the Phases of Operation

and CONPLAN. This planning effort forms the basis for future crisis action planning and provides good spectrum operations practice during exercises.

(2) Deter. During the deter phase, the emphasis should be placed on setting the conditions for joint operations in the seize the initiative and dominate phases. During the deter phase, the preponderance of military forces may be comprised of force deterrence options based on the existing OPLAN and special operations forces. The JFMO/JSME should be prepared to coordinate with these forces to fulfill their spectrum requirements.

(3) Seize the Initiative

(a) Considerations for seizing the initiative shift the JEMSMO focus from HNC to SM and frequency assignment. Joint reception, staging, onward movement, and integration, along with maintaining unit integrity, are additional considerations of seizing the initiative, which may be executed as a forcible entry operation. Forcible entry operations are complex and risky and require JEMSMO to enable early superiority in the information environment, which is critical to the success of joint operations. JSIR will also become a predominant function during this phase as elements and organizations are realigned and maneuvered to accomplish the mission.

(b) Coordination for staging areas is an often overlooked aspect of operations. Typically these staging areas are congested, and spectrum support may be very limited. Many units use staging areas to test equipment before actual operations, and congestion can lead to substantial frequency interference in addition to safety considerations of HERO, HERP, and HERF. EMSMs will need to provide increased assistance in staging area.

(4) Dominate. The dominate phase largely centers on SM and FM for forces in combat operations. Major operations generally require greater SM than small-scale operations because the JSME must constantly be aware of which elements are the focus of the main effort. As major operations progress, the shift in priorities may drive rapid spectrum allotment changes to support the main effort while ensuring both support and rear areas have spectrum support. Smaller operations generally allow for more efficient frequency reuse, provided forces have sufficient geographical separation. During both types of operations, the JSME will work with the JFC to mitigate the effects of adversary actions. JSIR in this phase is ongoing to ensure all joint functions' spectrum-dependent capabilities are maximized.

(5) Stabilize. While the focus of JEMSMO in the seize the initiative and dominate phases was on SM, FM, and JSIR, the stability phase will rely gradually more on the HNC as combat operations conclude. The JFMO/JSME will begin support of HN efforts to develop and implement national spectrum policy once the situation begins to stabilize.

(6) Enable Civil Authority

(a) HNC is the focus of this phase in addition to redeployment considerations. The JFMO/JSME should ensure that sufficient spectrum resources are retained in order to support redeployment operations. Enabling civil authority is a continuation of the stabilize phase. The JFMO/JSME will continue to work with the HN or organization that will assume responsibility for the spectrum. This process can be as simple as providing a list of frequency assignments to the incoming SM authority or involve much coordination and bureaucratic maneuvering.

(b) The incoming SM authority may require assistance in understanding the methodology used in making, documenting, and managing spectrum use. Any assistance (e.g., training, reference documents, frequency assignment information) provided to personnel outside of the USG requires a foreign disclosure evaluation and authorization. This evaluation and determination is usually a lengthy process and should be initiated as soon as the situation allows. The JSME's primary concern is to make sure that only information that is authorized for release outside of the DOD is provided. This determination must be coordinated through the JTF J-2.

2. Service Perspectives

The unique functionality of each of the Services promotes a different perspective of how to conduct JEMSMO. While these unique perspectives influence and dictate how they train and organize, successful JEMSMO requires that the Services operate in unison following a common construct.

a. **Air Force.** The Air Force mission is to fly, fight, and win, in air, space, and cyberspace. JEMSMO is a function needed to preplan and dynamically handle any required changes to what frequencies are allocated to whom, where, and when. There are spectrum tools that are used for allocating spectrum usage for a mission to assure minimum self-interference, maximize frequency reuse in adjacent geographic areas, and assure compliance with spectrum rules.

b. **Army**

(1) The Army's operational concept is seizing, retaining, and exploiting the initiative with speed, shock, surprise, depth, simultaneity, and endurance. The operational concept depends on flexible combinations of Army capabilities (combined arms) and joint capabilities (joint interdependence) integrated across the full spectrum of operations through mission command.

(2) JEMSMO supports this operational concept by enabling the synchronization of lethal and nonlethal attacks against targets in support of operational and tactical ground, air, cyberspace, and space operations. Synchronization is achieved by ensuring that JEMSMO is integral to operations in support of the ground scheme of maneuver, using centralized control and decentralized execution functions performed by parallel communications systems and procedures at all echelons.

(3) This requires the Army to have freedom of movement while operating within the EMOE. This is important because maneuver operations are highly dynamic with ground and airborne vehicles providing on-the-move communications and retransmission over a wide area. Current spectrum operations tools are not agile enough to fully accommodate these operations. It is therefore incumbent upon operators to fully understand the

commander's intent in order to anticipate and take appropriate actions to support the scheme of maneuver.

(4) Cross-Service coordination, synchronized with Army combat operations, is essential to the success of joint operations. Joint planning and continuous, effective coordination are critical to synchronizing JEMSMO capabilities and generating joint combat power at the critical time and place in battle. The Army provides and requires cross-Service coordination when and where needed to achieve the combat objectives and operational goals of the JFC.

c. **Marine Corps**

(1) Access to the EMS is fundamental to all Marine Corps missions spanning all joint functions (i.e., C2, intelligence, fires, maneuver, logistics, and force protection). Consideration of the EMS and operational environment is critical to acquisition, operations, and sustainment, and must continually be evaluated across the strategic, operational, and tactical planning levels of the Marine air-ground task force to ensure effective employment in the numerous and various locations in which the Marine Corps deploys.

(2) Within the Marine Corps CONOPS, JEMSMO supports the JFC by effectively and efficiently managing the EMS in order to ensure that the Marine Corps provides equipment, capabilities, and services to the operating forces and supporting establishment that enable commanders to plan for, coordinate, deconflict, and utilize spectrum-dependent equipment, systems, and capabilities in the successful completion of their assigned missions.

d. **Navy**

(1) JEMSMO supports the Navy's operational concept across the air, land, maritime, and space domains through the use of electronics and the EMS to store, modify, and exchange data via networked systems and associated physical infrastructures. JEMSMO supports this operational concept by enabling the flexible combinations of Navy, Marine Corps, and joint capabilities to be integrated across the full spectrum of operations through mission command. Navy provides a central operational authority for networks, cryptology/SIGINT, IO, cyberspace, EW, and space in support of forces afloat and ashore. Navy will establish emphasis on defense for information assurance and operational framework to assure Navy's ability to command and control its operational forces in any environment. Simultaneously, Navy must achieve and sustain the ability to navigate and maneuver freely in cyberspace and the RF spectrum on command, and in coordination with joint, allied, and Navy commanders.

(2) Numerous spectrum operational tools are being used to support the warfighter. While they are not responsive enough to fully accommodate dynamic military operations, naval operators and planners must understand and react quickly to the needs of the commander and the mission and operate quickly and effectively within a joint environment.

(3) Another major responsibility is providing effective communications planning for the JFC. This is critical for supporting the commanders' requests for required radio and/or interagency frequency approvals. Users should ensure that interoperability and coordination

for all their assigned communications capabilities. Users must understand current spectrum operation scenarios in order to fully support the fleet. Understanding JEMSMO for today's EM operations will provide successful operations in any environment.

e. **National Guard**

(1) The NG provides mission-ready military forces (Army and Air components) to assist local, state, and national authorities in times of emergencies, incidents of national significance, HD, and CS operations. The sheer variety of missions makes the efficient use of JEMSMO extremely important.

(2) The additional requirement for communications interoperability with local first responders, state and federal civilian agencies, and Title 10, USC, forces makes JEMSMO considerations all the more important. The NG normally serves under the control of the state governor (Title 32, USC). When federalized (i.e., Title 10, USC, status), they serve under their assigned CCMD—usually USNORTHCOM and United States Pacific Command. While in Title 32, USC, status, ARNG units request spectrum support through their parent commands from the JFHQ-State EMSM, who in turn requests spectrum support from AFMO-CONUS. If federalized, the ARNG will be required to submit frequency requests either directly to the supported CCMD or Army Forces Command in the case of predeployment training.

(3) NG units may have a blend of both tactical and commercial systems. When processing NG frequency requests, special attention should be paid to the requests to ensure that only federally funded systems are given assignments. Typically, these are tactical systems such as single-channel ground and airborne radio system and other systems, tactical HF, tactical ultrahigh frequency satellite communications, etc. Commercial systems procured with state funding may not have spectrum certification and are not spectrum supportable through DOD channels.

CHAPTER VII
MULTINATIONAL OPERATIONS

1. Introduction

Normally, when a multinational force is formed, there will be no previously agreed upon spectrum operations procedures. This creates difficulties and causes delays with the planning, coordination, management, and execution of spectrum operations. Spectrum operations procedures used within alliances should be agreed upon in the earliest stages of planning.

2. Considerations in Multinational Operations

a. Recent operations, ENDURING FREEDOM and IRAQI FREEDOM, demonstrate the need for aligning DOD spectrum operations policies and procedures with those of US and multinational partners. US EMSMs must be prepared to integrate US spectrum requirements into a multinational spectrum-use plan to support the mission. The development of specific procedures to support this requirement is made more difficult because of concise security guidance, differences in the level of training, different automation tools, and some language and terminology barriers.

b. A CONOPS must be developed in order to execute JEMSMO in a multinational environment. Establishing an acceptable CONOPS for EMS operations may be a difficult and protracted process. OPLANs and communications support plans should address coordination among spectrum users to achieve effective exchange of information, elimination of duplication of effort, and mutual support. Activities that should be addressed within the CONOPS include the organizational structure and processes used in a multinational environment, security concerns, spectrum data exchange requirements, and spectrum tools.

c. A spectrum operations structure should be established for each operation. The structure should identify the location and responsibilities of spectrum operators. Multinational operations will generally be conducted one of two ways: either all forces operate in the same area, or the operational environment will be subdivided and national forces will be given responsibility for particular geographic areas. The first is generally the most complicated because the number and types of equipment will vary greatly between the multinational forces. Even when the operational environment is divided, it will be necessary to plan and coordinate among adjacent spectrum users.

d. The JTF foreign disclosure officer, integrated into the JSME, must provide foreign disclosure guidelines early enough in the operational planning phases to facilitate the flow of information. For JEMSMO to be executed properly, spectrum operators must have a complete picture of their EMOE to populate spectrum databases and management tools. Due to security considerations related to the use or employment of some equipment that nations employ for military intelligence or other sensitive functions, some equipment information may not be releasable to all countries involved in an operation. This typically causes problems with accurate spectrum deconfliction. For this reason, all spectrum releasability/classification information must be distributed and available at all levels. This should apply to all multinational EMS information, to include the JRFL, JCEOI, etc.

e. The information exchange format should be agreed to as early as possible in the planning process. DOD forces should advocate the use of DOD data exchange standards to minimize the time and effort necessary to build their spectrum databases. As much as possible, forces should agree upon the JEMSMO tools used to facilitate operational issues such as interference resolution and reporting, constructing restricted frequency lists for EW operations, and constructing and producing operating instructions.

f. Multinational spectrum operators may not be trained to the same standards as US EMSMs. They have different automation capabilities, responsibilities, and national requirements. US EMSMs can be expected to lead the overall database management effort and provide training to their allied counterparts when DOD automation tools are used. Commanders should resource the allied/multinational spectrum office with experienced spectrum operators commensurate with the size and scope of the operation.

For more information on multinational operations, see CJCSM 3320.01B, Joint Operations in the Electromagnetic Battlespace, *and ACP 190(C),* Guide to Spectrum Management in Military Operations.

3. Considerations for Foreign Humanitarian Assistance/Disaster Relief

Foreign humanitarian assistance is defined as DOD activities, normally in support of the United States Agency for International Development or Department of State, conducted outside the United States and its territories to relieve or reduce human suffering, disease, hunger, or privation. Military forces may be deployed to provide aid to the civil administration in a mix of civil and military humanitarian relief agencies. The civil administration (if one exists) should provide an SM framework for the deployed military force. Much of the JEMSMO would focus on HNC and ensuring that disruption to civil systems would be minimized through coordination. Where administration does not exist, this responsibility may be delegated to a lead military force as directed by the CCDR. The support would be much more like a forced entry operation, and the JFMO/JSME would need to develop and implement the spectrum plan to support operations.

APPENDIX A
REFERENCES

The development of JP 6-01 is based upon the following primary references.

1. Department of Defense

a. DODD 3000.3, *Policy for Nonlethal Weapons.*

b. DODD 3222.3, *DOD Electromagnetic Environmental Effects (E3) Program.*

c. DODI 4650.01, *Policy and Procedures for Management and Use of the Electromagnetic Spectrum.*

2. Chairman of the Joint Chiefs of Staff

a. CJCSI 3320.01C, *Electromagnetic Spectrum Use in Joint Military Operations.*

b. CJCSI 3320.02D.1, *Classified Supplement to the Joint Spectrum Interference Resolution (JSIR) Procedures.*

c. CJCSI 3320.02E, *Joint Spectrum Interference Resolution (JSIR).*

d. CJCSI 3320.03B, *Joint Communications Electronic Operating Instructions.*

e. CJCSI 6212.01E, *Interoperability and Supportability of Information Technology and National Security Systems.*

f. CJCSI 6232.01D, *Link 16 Spectrum Deconfliction.*

g. CJCSM 3212.02C, *Performing Electronic Attacks in the US and Canada for Tests, Training, and Exercises.*

h. CJCSM 3320.01B, *Joint Operations in the Electromagnetic Battlespace.*

i. CJCSM 3320.02C, *Joint Spectrum Interference Resolution (JSIR) Procedures.*

j. JP 1-02, *DOD Dictionary of Military and Associated Terms.*

k. JP 3-0, *Joint Operations.*

l. JP 3-11, *Operations in Chemical, Biological, Radiological, and Nuclear (CBRN) Environments.*

m. JP 3-13.1, *Electronic Warfare.*

n. JP 3-13.2, *Military Information Support Operations.*

o. JP 3-41, *Chemical, Biological, Radiological, and Nuclear Consequence Management.*

p. JP 6-0, *Joint Communications System.*

q. MCEB PUB 7, *Frequency Resource Record System (FRRS) Standard Frequency Action Format (SFAF).*

3. Multinational and Multi-Service

a. ACP 190 NATO SUPP-2 (C), *NATO Guide to Spectrum Management in Military Operations.*

b. ACP 190(B), *NATO Guide to Spectrum Management in Military Operations.*

c. ACP 190(C), *Guide to Spectrum Management in Military Operations.*

d. ACP 190 US SUPP-1(D), *Guide to Frequency Planning.*

e. ACP 194, *Policy for the Coordination of Military Radio Frequency Allocations and Assignments Between Cooperating Nations.*

f. Field Manual 3-11.4/MCWP 3-37.2/NTTP 3-11.27/AFTTP(I) 3-2.46, *Multi-Service Tactics, Techniques, and Procedures for Nuclear, Biological, and Chemical (NBC) Protection.*

4. Air Force Publications

a. AFDD 3-13, *Information Operations.*

b. AFDD 3-13.1, *Electronic Warfare.*

c. AFDD 6-0, *Command and Control.*

d. AFI 10-707, *Spectrum Interference Resolution Program.*

e. AFI 33-106, *Managing High Frequency Radios, Personal Wireless Communication Systems, and the Military Affiliate Radio System.*

f. AFI 33-118, *Electromagnetic Spectrum Management.*

g. AFMAN 91-201, *Explosives Safety Standards.*

h. AFOSH STD 48-9, *Radio Frequency Radiation (RFR).*

5. Army Publications

a. AR 1-1, *Planning, Programming, Budgeting, and Execution System.*

b. AR 5-12, *Army Management of the Electromagnetic Spectrum.*

c. AR 25-1, *Army Knowledge Management and Information Technology.*

d. AR 380-5, *Department of the Army Information Security Program.*

e. Field Manual 6-02.70, *Army Electromagnetic Spectrum Operations.*

f. Field Manual 3-36, *Electronic Warfare in Operations.*

6. Marine Corps Publications

a. MCO 2400.2, *Marine Corps Management and Use of the Electromagnetic Spectrum.*

b. MCO 2410.2B, *Electromagnetic Environmental Effects (E3) Control Program.*

c. MCO 3430.2, *Policy for Electronic Warfare.*

d. MCWP 2-22, *Signals Intelligence.*

e. MCWP 3-40.3, *MAGTF Communications System.*

7. Navy Publications

a. NTTP 3-13.10, *Submarine Electronic Warfare.*

b. NTTP 3-13.14, *Surface Electronic Warfare Guide.*

c. NTTP 3-51.1, *Navy Electronic Warfare.*

d. NWP 3-13, *Navy Information Operations.*

e. NWP 3-32, *Maritime Operations at the Operational Level of War.*

f. Naval Air Systems Command Instruction 2400.1, *Electromagnetic Environmental Effects and Spectrum Supportability Policy and Procedures.*

g. Naval Sea Systems Command S9407-AA-GYD-010/OP-3840, *Electromagnetic Compatibility Criteria for Navy Systems.*

h. Technical Manual (TM) 5.13.2-04, *Afloat Electromagnetic Spectrum Planning and Management.*

i. TM SWDG 3-51.2-01, *Surface Ship Electronic Attack.*

8. US Coast Guard Publications

a. Coast Guard Publication 1, *US Coast Guard: America's Maritime Guardian.*

b. Commandant, United States Coast Guard Instruction (COMDTINST) M2400.1, *Spectrum Management Policy and Procedures.*

c. COMDTINST M4200.19, *Coast Guard Acquisition Procedures.*

9. Military Standards and Handbooks

a. Military Standard (MIL-STD)-461F, *DOD Interface Standard Requirements for the Control of Electromagnetic Interference Characteristics of Subsystems and Equipment.*

b. MIL-STD-464A, *DOD Interface Standard Electromagnetic Environmental Effects Requirements for Systems.*

APPENDIX B
ADMINISTRATIVE INSTRUCTIONS

1. User Comments

Users in the field are highly encouraged to submit comments on this publication to: Joint Staff J-7, Deputy Director, Joint and Coalition Warfighting, Joint and Coalition Warfighting Center, ATTN: Joint Doctrine Support Division, 116 Lake View Parkway, Suffolk, VA 23435-2697. These comments should address content (accuracy, usefulness, consistency, and organization), writing, and appearance.

2. Authorship

The lead agent for this publication is the US Army. The Joint Staff doctrine sponsor for this publication is the Deputy Director, Command, Control, Communications, and Computer Systems.

3. Change Recommendations

a. Recommendations for urgent changes to this publication should be submitted electronically to the lead agent, with information copies sent to the Joint Staff J-7 Joint Education and Doctrine Division and the Joint Staff J-7, Deputy Director, Joint and Coalition Warfighting, Joint and Coalition Warfighting Center, Joint Doctrine Support Division.

b. Routine changes should be submitted to electronically to the Deputy Director, Joint and Coalition Warfighting, Joint and Coalition Warfighting Center, Joint Doctrine Support Division, and info the lead agent and the Director for Joint Force Development, J-7/JEDD.

c. When a Joint Staff directorate submits a proposal to the Chairman of the Joint Chiefs of Staff that would change source document information reflected in this publication, that directorate will include a proposed change to this publication as an enclosure to its proposal. The Services and other organizations are requested to notify the Joint Staff/J-7 when changes to source documents reflected in this publication are initiated.

4. Distribution of Publications

Local reproduction is authorized and access to unclassified publications is unrestricted. However, access to and reproduction authorization for classified JPs must be IAW DOD 5200.1-R, *Information Security Program.*

5. Distribution of Electronic Publications

a. Joint Staff J-7 will not print copies of JPs for distribution. Electronic versions are available on JDEIS at https://jdeis.js.mil (NIPRNET), and https://jdeis.js.smil.mil (SIPRNET) and on the JEL at http://www.dtic.mil/doctrine (NIPRNET).

b. Only approved JPs and joint test publications are releasable outside the CCMDs, Services, and Joint Staff. Release of any classified JP to foreign governments or foreign nationals must be requested through the local embassy (Defense Attaché Office) to DIA Foreign Liaison/IE-3, 200 MacDill Blvd., Joint Base Anacostia-Bolling, Washington, DC 20340-5100.

   c. CD-ROM. Upon request of a joint doctrine development community member, the Joint Staff J-7 will produce and deliver one CD-ROM with current JPs.

GLOSSARY
PART I—ABBREVIATIONS AND ACRONYMS

A-2	intelligence staff officer (Air Force)
A-3	operations staff officer (Air Force)
A-6	communications staff officer (Air Force)
AAG	aeronautical assignment group
ACOS	assistant chief of staff
ACP	Allied communications publication
AFI	Air Force instruction
AFSMO	Air Force Spectrum Management Office
ANG	Air National Guard
AOI	area of interest
AOR	area of responsibility
AR	Army regulation
ARNG	Army National Guard
ASM	Army Spectrum Manager
ASMO	Army Spectrum Management Office
C2	command and control
CBRN	chemical, biological, radiological, and nuclear
CCDR	combatant commander
CCEB	Combined Communications–Electronics Board
CCMD	combatant command
C-E	communications–electronics
CG-652	Coast Guard Spectrum Management and Telecommunications Policy Division
CIO	chief information officer
CJCSI	Chairman of the Joint Chiefs of Staff instruction
CJCSM	Chairman of the Joint Chiefs of Staff manual
CNO	computer network operations
COMDTINST	Commandant of the Coast Guard instruction
CONOPS	concept of operations
CONPLAN	concept plan
CONUS	continental United States
DIA	Defense Intelligence Agency
DISA	Defense Information Systems Agency
DOD	Department of Defense
DODD	Department of Defense directive
DODI	Department of Defense instruction
DON	Department of the Navy
DSCA	defense support of civil authorities
DSO	Defense Spectrum Organization

E3	electromagnetic environmental effects
EA	electronic attack
EM	electromagnetic
EME	electromagnetic environment
EMI	electromagnetic interference
EMOE	electromagnetic operational environment
EMP	electromagnetic pulse
EMS	electromagnetic spectrum
EOB	electromagnetic order of battle
EP	electronic protection
EW	electronic warfare
EWC	electronic warfare cell
EWO	electronic warfare officer
FAS	frequency assignment subcommittee
FCC	Federal Communications Commission
FM	frequency management
G-2	Army or Marine Corps component intelligence staff officer (Army division or higher staff, Marine Corps brigade or higher staff)
G-3	Army or Marine Corps component operations staff officer (Army division or higher staff, Marine Corps brigade or higher staff)
G-6	signal staff officer (Army)
GCC	geographic combatant commander
HD	homeland defense
HEMP	high-altitude electromagnetic pulse
HERF	hazards of electromagnetic radiation to fuels
HERO	hazards of electromagnetic radiation to ordnance
HERP	hazards of electromagnetic radiation to personnel
HF	high frequency
HN	host nation
HNC	host-nation coordination
HQMC	Headquarters, Marine Corps
Hz	hertz
IAW	in accordance with
IC	intelligence community
IGO	intergovernmental organization
IO	information operations
IRAC	Interdepartment Radio Advisory Committee (DOC)
ITU	International Telecommunications Union

J-2	intelligence directorate of a joint staff
J-3	operations directorate of a joint staff
J-5	plans directorate of a joint staff
J-6	communications system directorate of a joint staff
JCCC	joint communications control center
JCEOI	joint communications–electronics operating instructions
JEMSMO	joint electromagnetic spectrum management operations
JEMSO	joint electromagnetic spectrum operations
JFC	joint force commander
JFHQ-State	joint force headquarters–state
JFMO	joint frequency management office
JFP	Joint Frequency Panel (MCEB)
JOPES	Joint Operation Planning and Execution System
JOPP	joint operation planning process
JP	joint publication
JRFL	joint restricted frequency list
JSC	Joint Spectrum Center
JSIR	joint spectrum interference resolution
JSME	joint spectrum management element
JTF	joint task force
MAG	military assignment group
MC	Military Committee (NATO)
MCEB	Military Communications–Electronics Board
MCO	Marine Corps order
METOC	meteorological and oceanographic
MILDEC	military deception
MILDEP	Military Department
MIL-STD	military standard
MISO	military information support operations
MNL	master net list
NATO	North Atlantic Treaty Organization
NAVCYBERFOR	Navy Cyber Forces
NETOPS	network operations
NG	National Guard
NGB	National Guard Bureau
NGO	nongovernmental organization
NMCSO	Navy and Marine Corps spectrum office
NMSC	Navy and Marine Corps Spectrum Center
NTIA	National Telecommunications and Information Administration
OASD(NII/CIO)	Office of the Assistant Secretary of Defense (Networks and Information Integration/Chief Information Officer)
OMC	Office of Military Cooperation

OPLAN	operation plan
OPSEC	operations security
OPTASK	operation task
OSM	Office of Spectrum Management (NTIA)
RF	radio frequency
SFAT	spectrum flyaway team
SIGINT	signals intelligence
SM	spectrum management
SMB	spectrum management branch
SOFA	status-of-forces agreement
SUPP	supplement
TV	television
UAS	unmanned aircraft system
USC	United States Code
USCG	United States Coast Guard
USG	United States Government
USLO	United States liaison office
USNORTHCOM	United States Northern Command
WG	working group

PART II—TERMS AND DEFINITIONS

bandwidth. None. (Approved for removal from JP 1-02.)

electromagnetic operational environment. The background electromagnetic environment and the friendly, neutral, and adversarial electromagnetic order of battle within the electromagnetic area of influence associated with a given operational area. Also called **EMOE.** (Approved for inclusion in JP 1-02.)

electromagnetic radiation. Radiation made up of oscillating electric and magnetic fields and propagated at the speed of light. (Approved for incorporation into JP 1-02.)

electromagnetic spectrum management. Planning, coordinating, and managing use of the electromagnetic spectrum through operational, engineering, and administrative procedures. (Approved for incorporation into JP 1-02.)

electronic line of sight. None. (Approved for removal from JP 1-02.)

joint electromagnetic spectrum management operations. Those interrelated functions of frequency management, host nation coordination, and joint spectrum inteference resolution that together enable the planning, management, and execution of operations within the electromagnetic operational environment during all phases of military operations. Also called **JEMSMO.** (Approved for inclusion in JP 1-02.)

joint electromagnetic spectrum operations. Those activities consisting of electronic warfare and joint electromagnetic spectrum management operations used to exploit, attack, protect, and manage the electromagnetic operational environment to achieve the commander's objectives. Also called **JEMSO.** (Approved for inclusion in JP 1-02.)

minimum obstruction clearance altitude. None. (Approved for removal from JP 1-02.)

minimum reception altitude. None. (Approved for removal from JP 1-02.)

multichannel. None. (Approved for removal from JP 1-02.)

multiplexer. None. (Approved for removal from JP 1-02.)

net control station. None. (Approved for removal from JP 1-02.)

signal-to-noise ratio. None. (Approved for removal from JP 1-02.)

technical characteristics. None. (Approved for removal from JP 1-02.)

JOINT DOCTRINE PUBLICATIONS HIERARCHY

JP 1
JOINT DOCTRINE
JP 1-0
PERSONNEL
JP 2-0
INTELLIGENCE
JP 3-0
OPERATIONS
JP 4-0
LOGISTICS
JP 5-0
PLANS
JP 6-0
COMMUNICATIONS SYSTEM

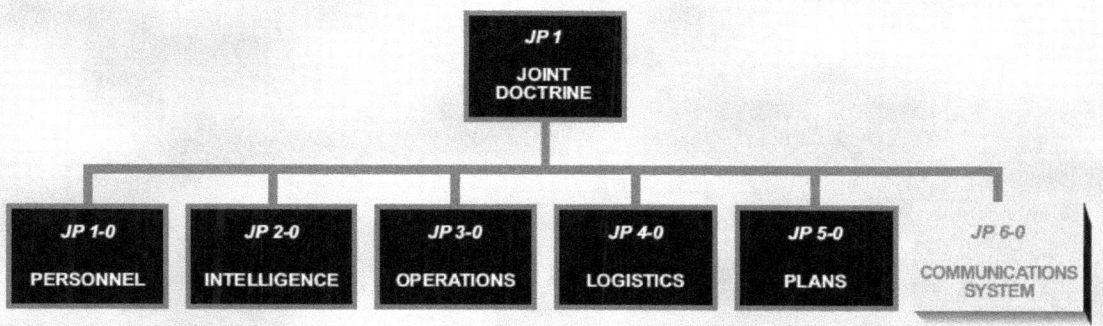

All joint publications are organized into a comprehensive hierarchy as shown in the chart above. **Joint Publication (JP) 6-01** is in the **Communications System** series of joint doctrine publications. The diagram below illustrates an overview of the development process:

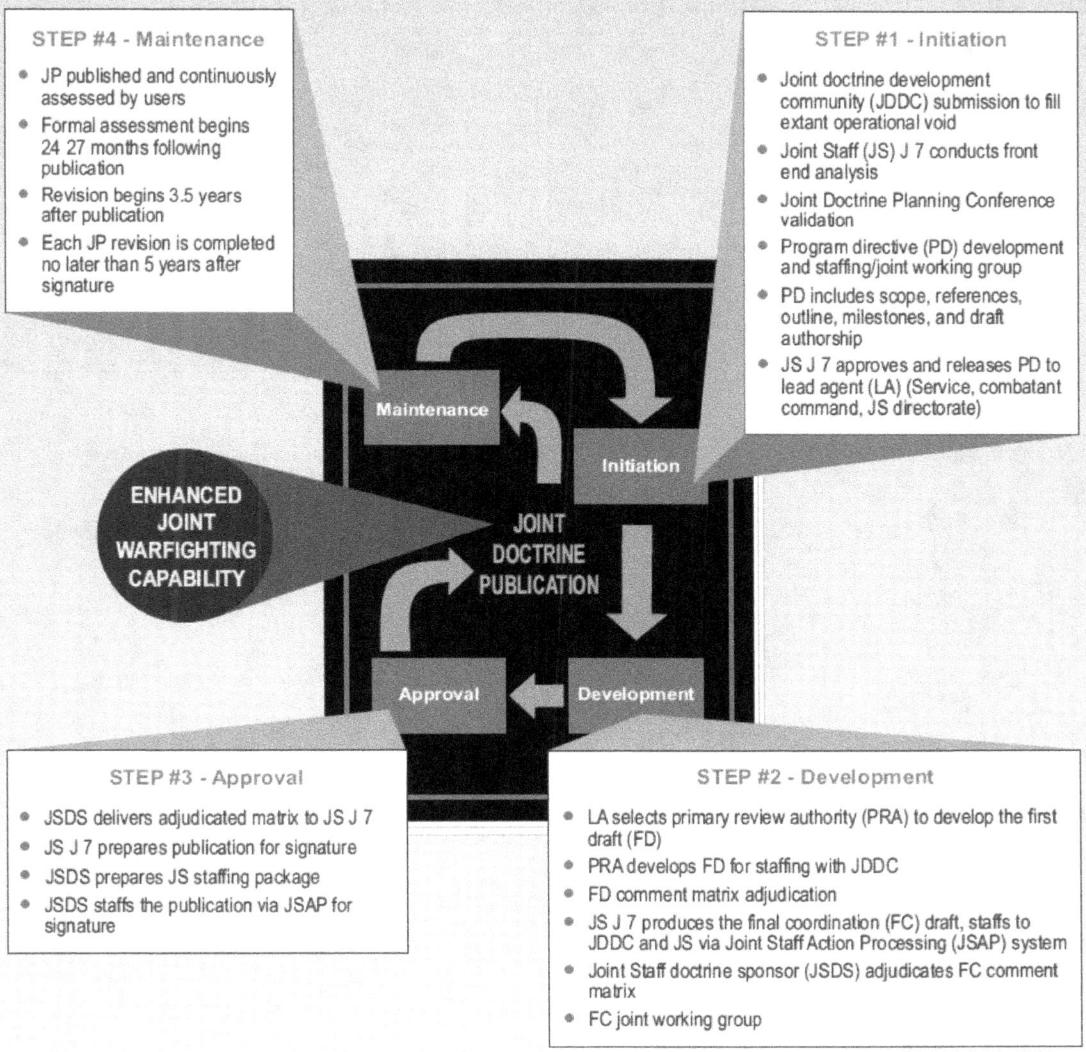

STEP #4 - Maintenance
JP published and continuously assessed by users
Formal assessment begins 24 27 months following publication
Revision begins 3.5 years after publication
Each JP revision is completed no later than 5 years after signature
STEP #1 - Initiation
Joint doctrine development community (JDDC) submission to fill extant operational void
Joint Staff (JS) J 7 conducts front end analysis
Joint Doctrine Planning Conference validation
Program directive (PD) development and staffing/joint working group
PD includes scope, references, outline, milestones, and draft authorship
JS J 7 approves and releases PD to lead agent (LA) (Service, combatant command, JS directorate)
Maintenance
Initiation
ENHANCED JOINT WARFIGHTING CAPABILITY
JOINT DOCTRINE PUBLICATION
Approval
Development
STEP #3 - Approval
JSDS delivers adjudicated matrix to JS J 7
JS J 7 prepares publication for signature
JSDS prepares JS staffing package
JSDS staffs the publication via JSAP for signature
STEP #2 - Development
LA selects primary review authority (PRA) to develop the first draft (FD)
PRA develops FD for staffing with JDDC
FD comment matrix adjudication
JS J 7 produces the final coordination (FC) draft, staffs to JDDC and JS via Joint Staff Action Processing (JSAP) system
Joint Staff doctrine sponsor (JSDS) adjudicates FC comment matrix
FC joint working group

www.ingramcontent.com/pod-product-compliance
Lightning Source LLC
Chambersburg PA
CBHW080315290526
45790CB00005B/2052